TO

Joan

FROM

With love at Easter 2021

DATE

INSPIRATIONAL *Hope*

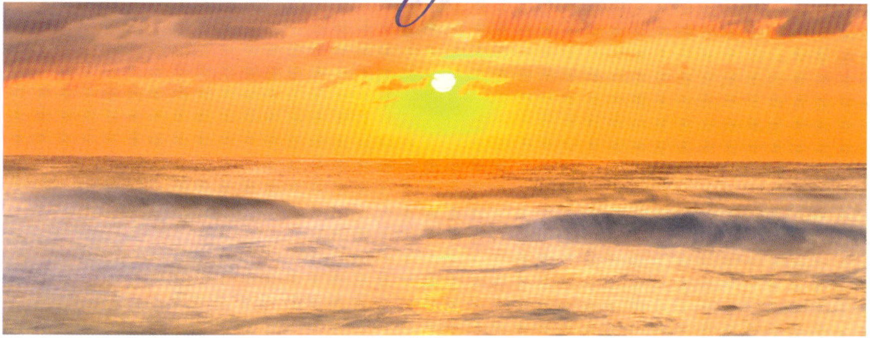

AUSTRALIAN PHOTOGRAPHS BY KEN DUNCAN

PANOGRAPHS®
PUBLISHING PTY LTD

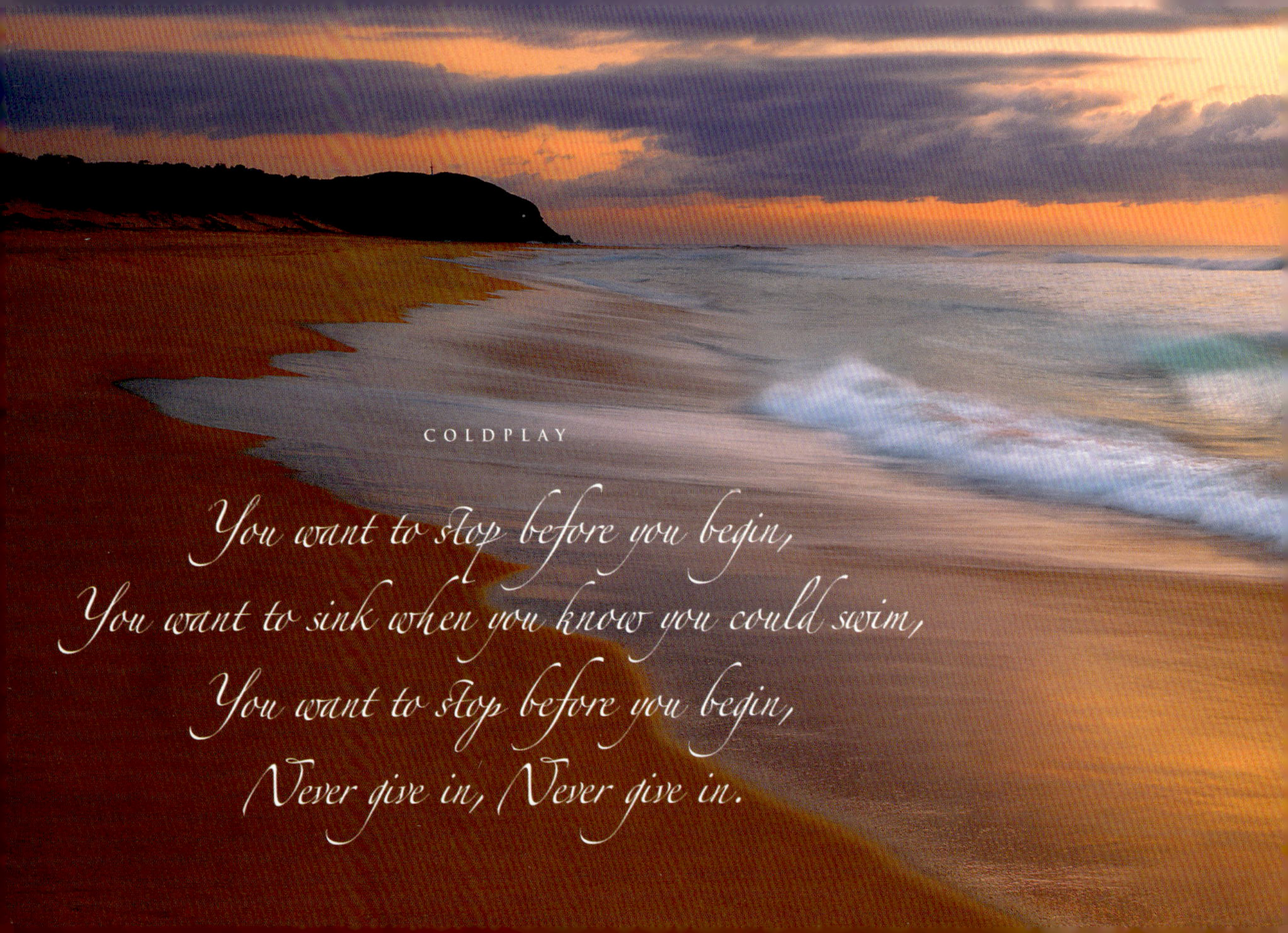
COLDPLAY
You want to stop before you begin,
You want to sink when you know you could swim,
You want to stop before you begin,
Never give in, Never give in.

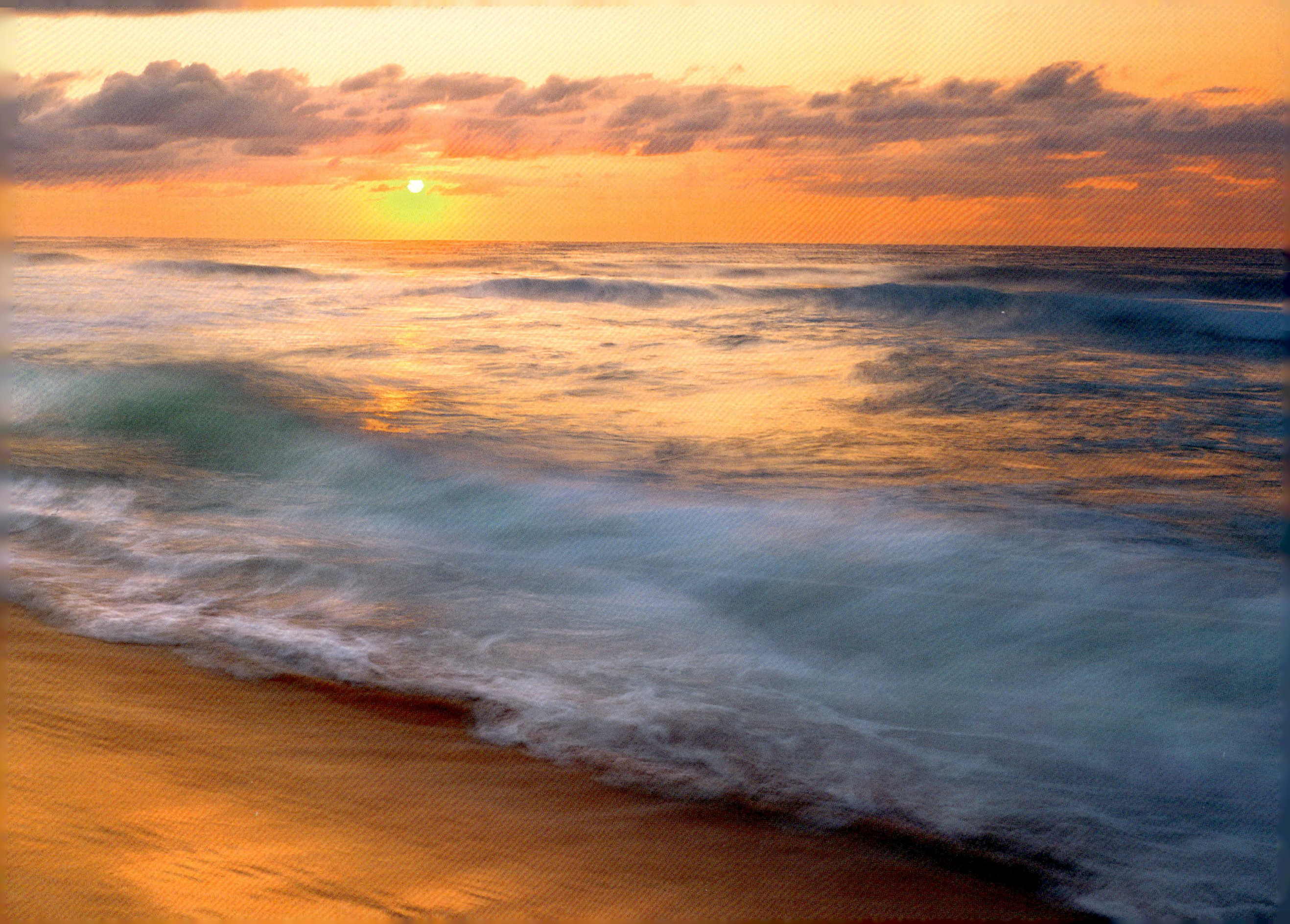

While there's life, there's hope. MARCUS TULLIUS CICERO

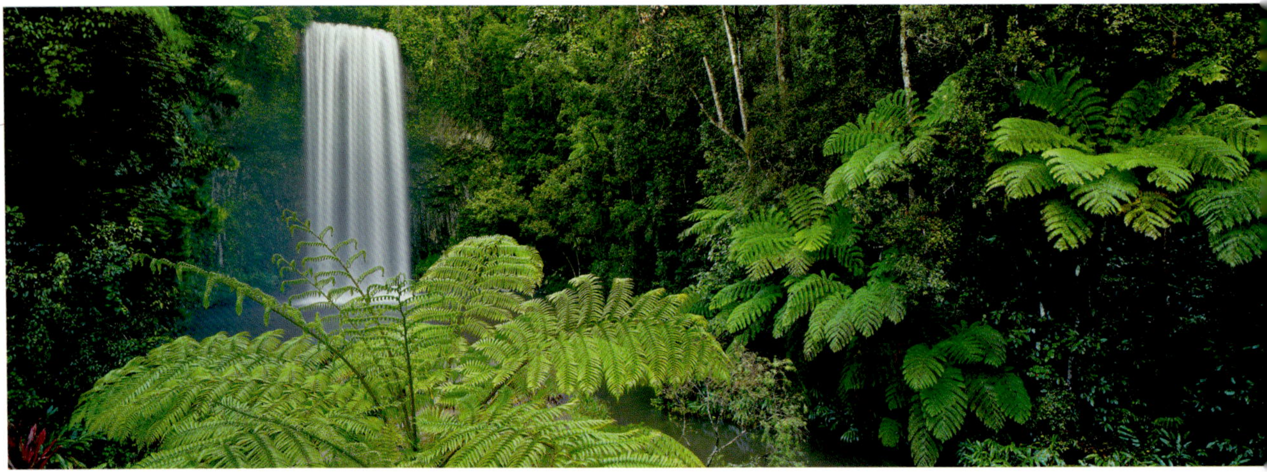

FRONT COVER *Let there be Joy, Sunflowers, NSW*
PREVIOUS PAGE *Sunrise, Wamberal Beach, NSW*
THIS PAGE *Majestic Beauty, Millaa Millaa Falls, Qld*

— INTRODUCTION —

Worry and fear have no nationality; they affect people all over the world. I have seen people try many ways of dealing with these afflictions but we need faith and hope to truly overcome despair.

As you reflect upon the beauty of creation in these photographs and ponder the accompanying quotes, I hope you will come to realise there is a power greater than any situation we may find ourselves in. If you will open your spirit to the Creator of our magnificent universe, you will find new hope and strength to face each new day and overcome life's challenges.

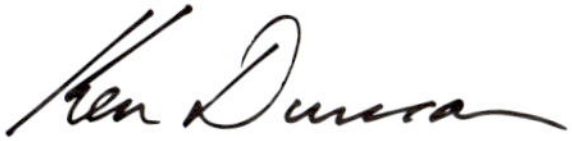

Walk on, walk on,
with hope in your heart,
and you'll never walk alone.

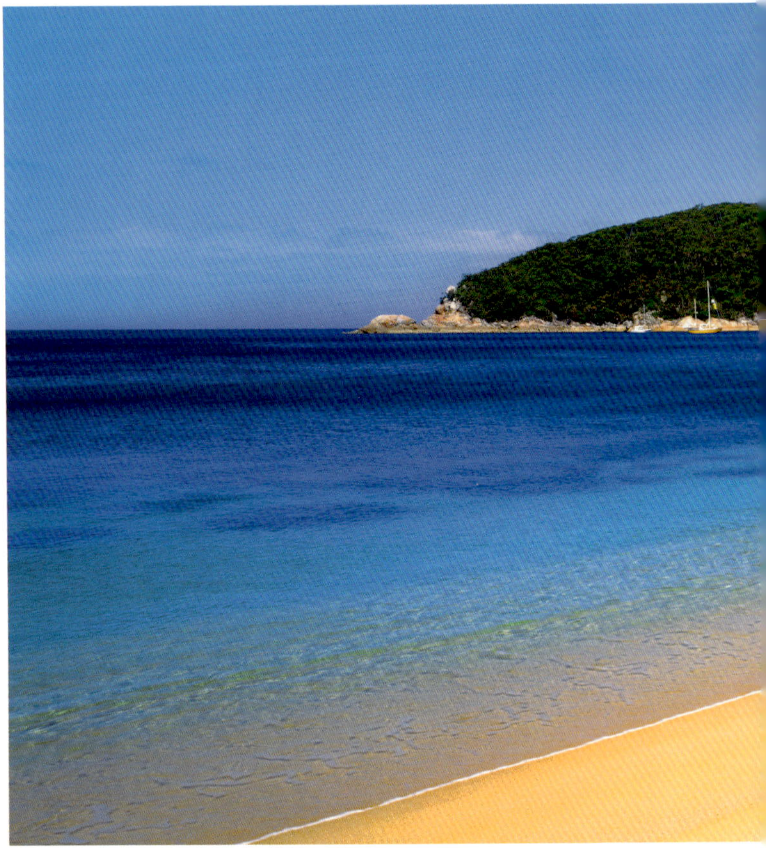

Refuge Cove, Wilson's Promontory, Vic

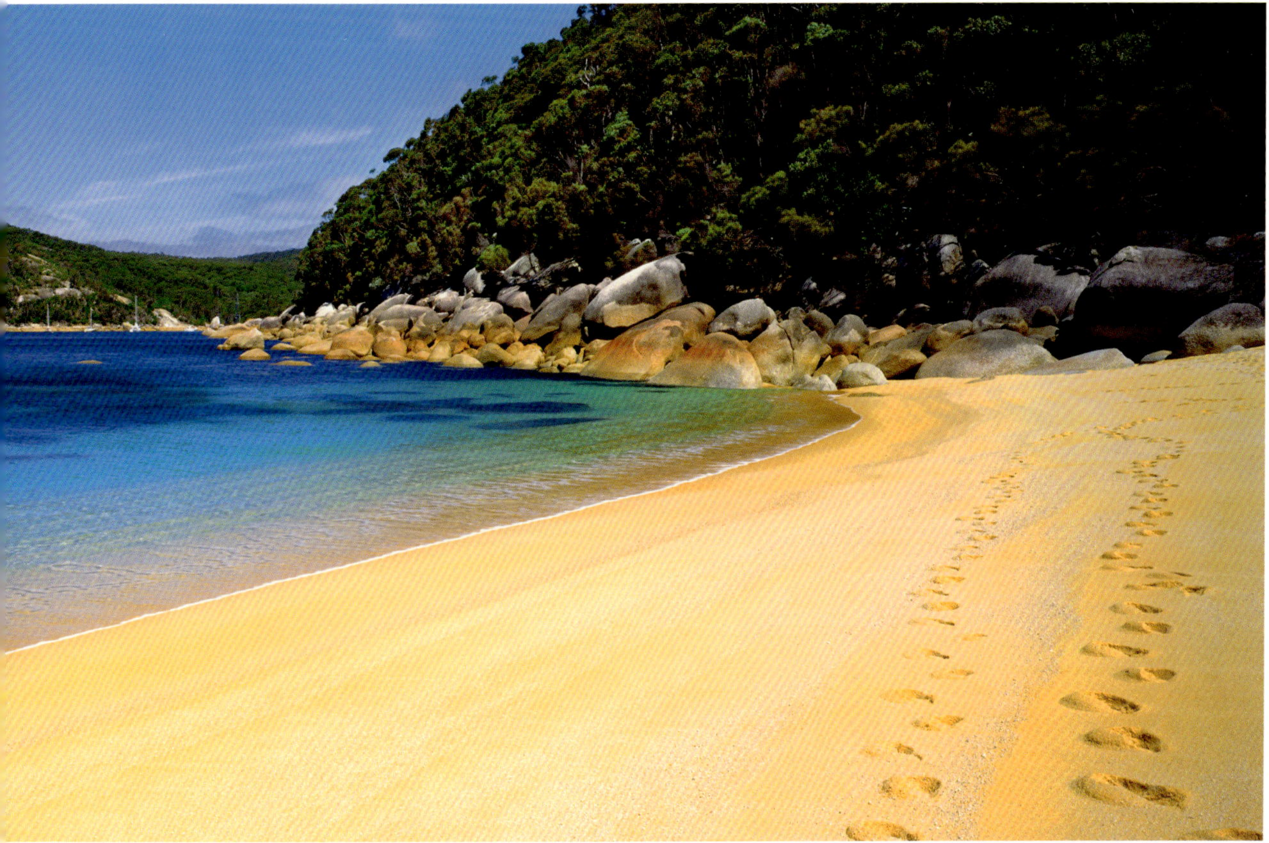

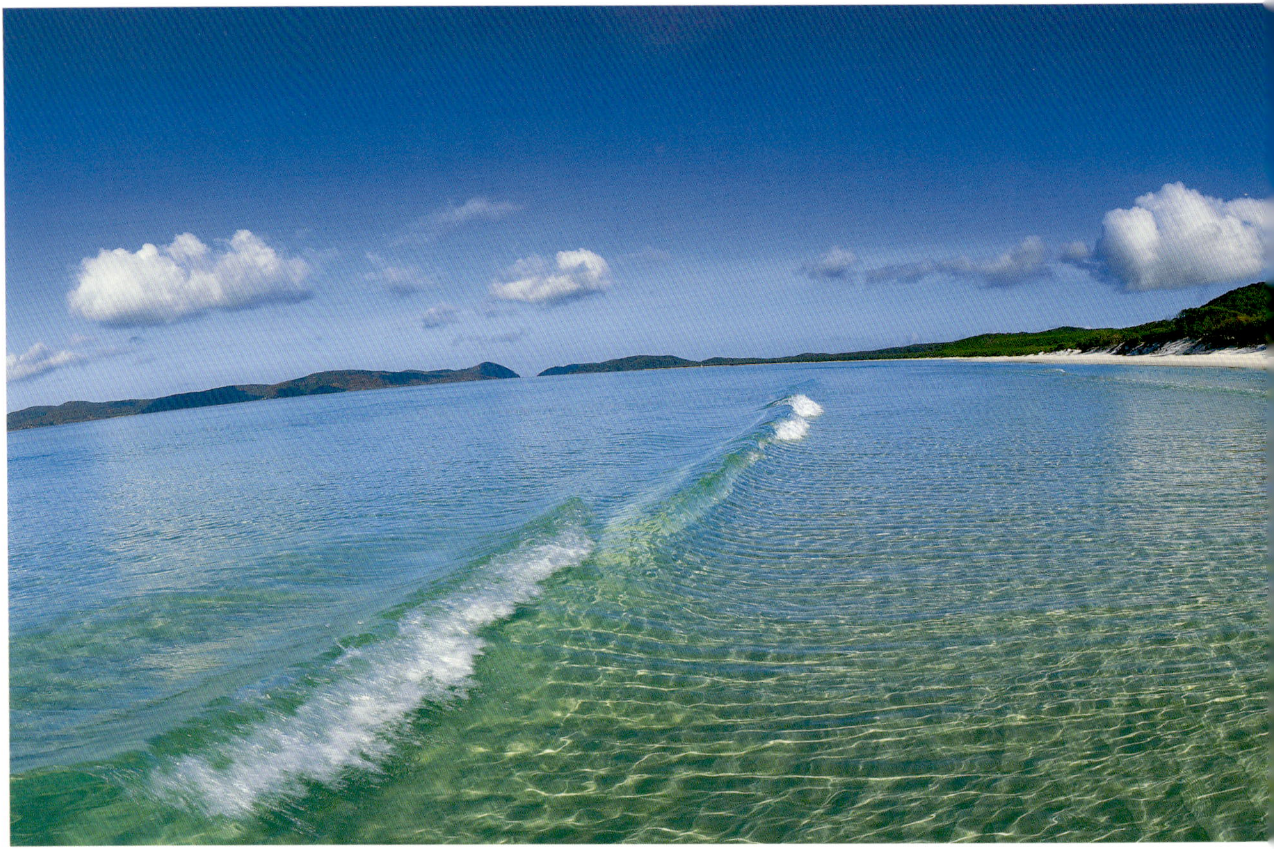

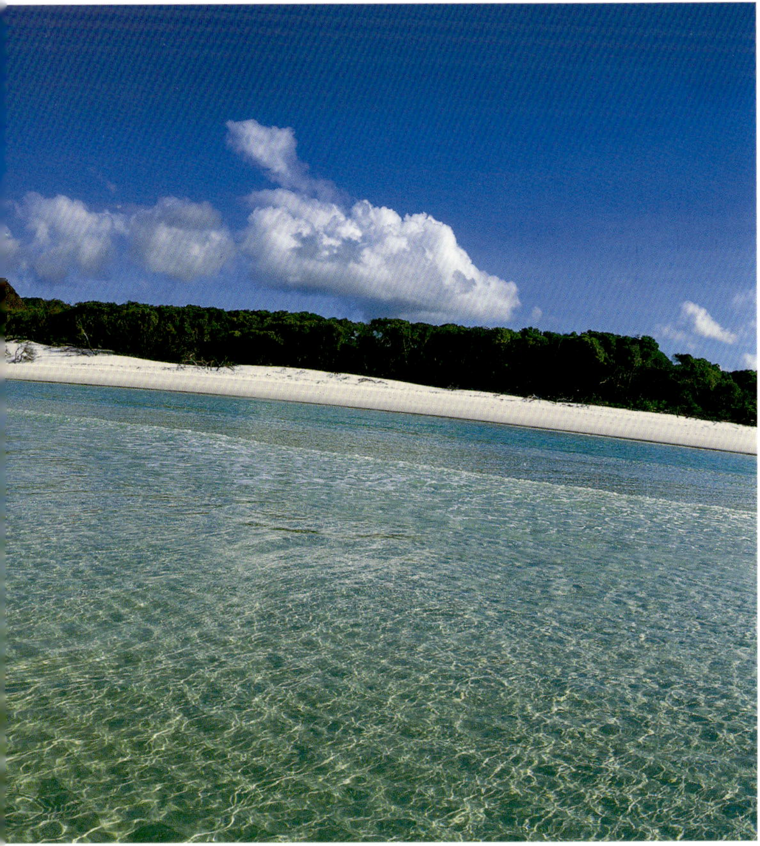

THOMAS FULLER

If it were not for hope,
the heart would break.

THIS PAGE
Whitehaven Beach, Qld

FOLLOWING PAGES
Piccaninny Creek, Purnululu National Park, WA

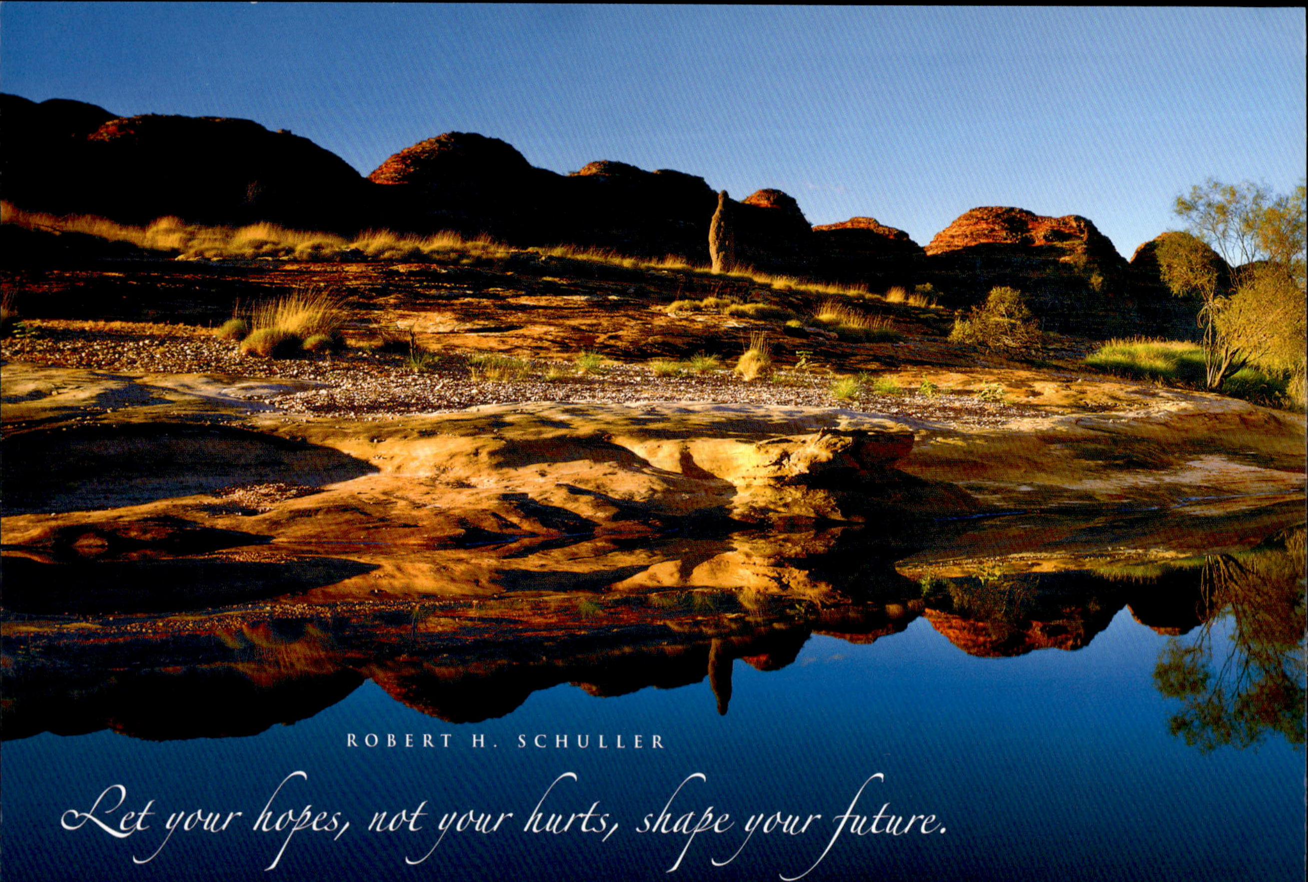
ROBERT H. SCHULLER
Let your hopes, not your hurts, shape your future.

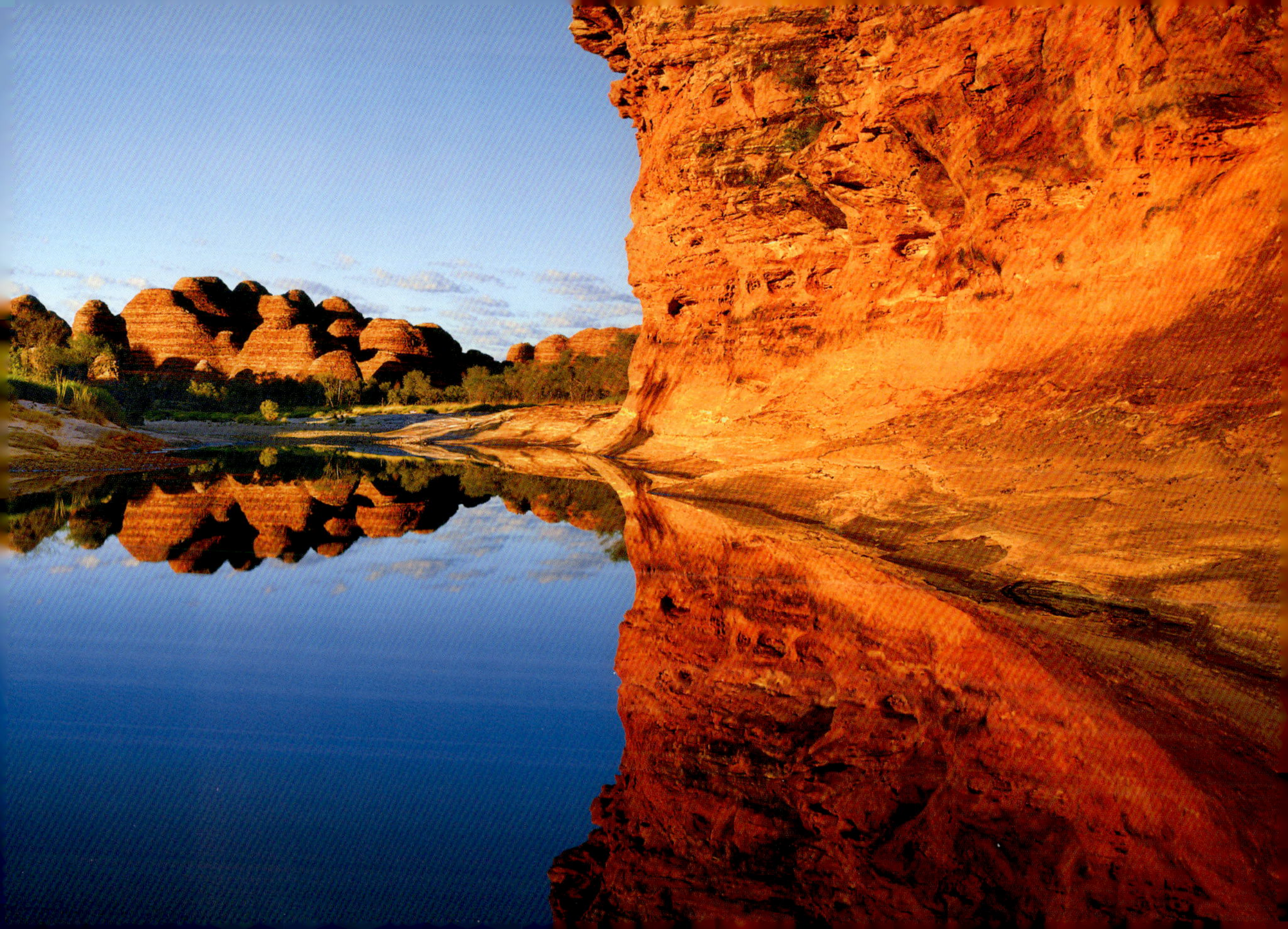

Hope is patience
with the lamp lit.

Sunrise, Boomerang Beach, NSW

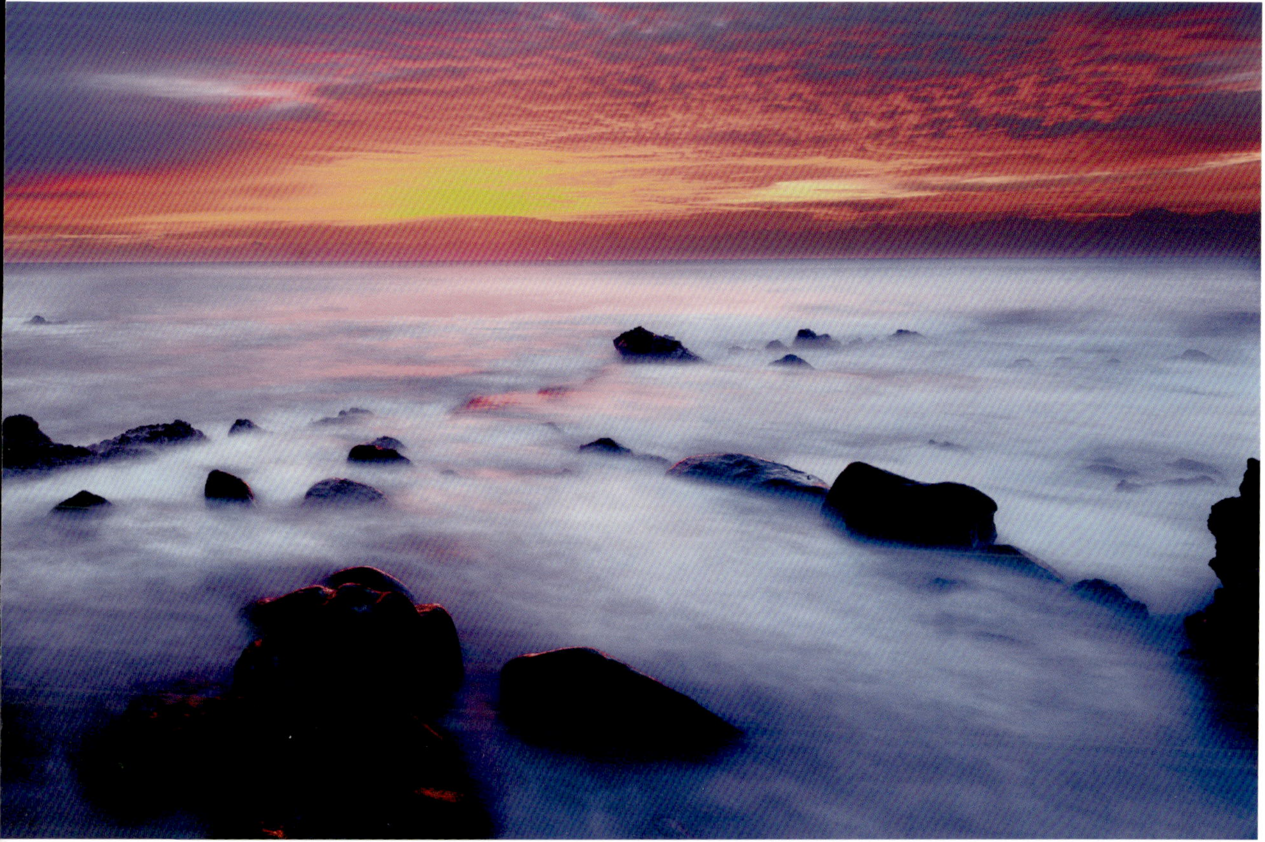

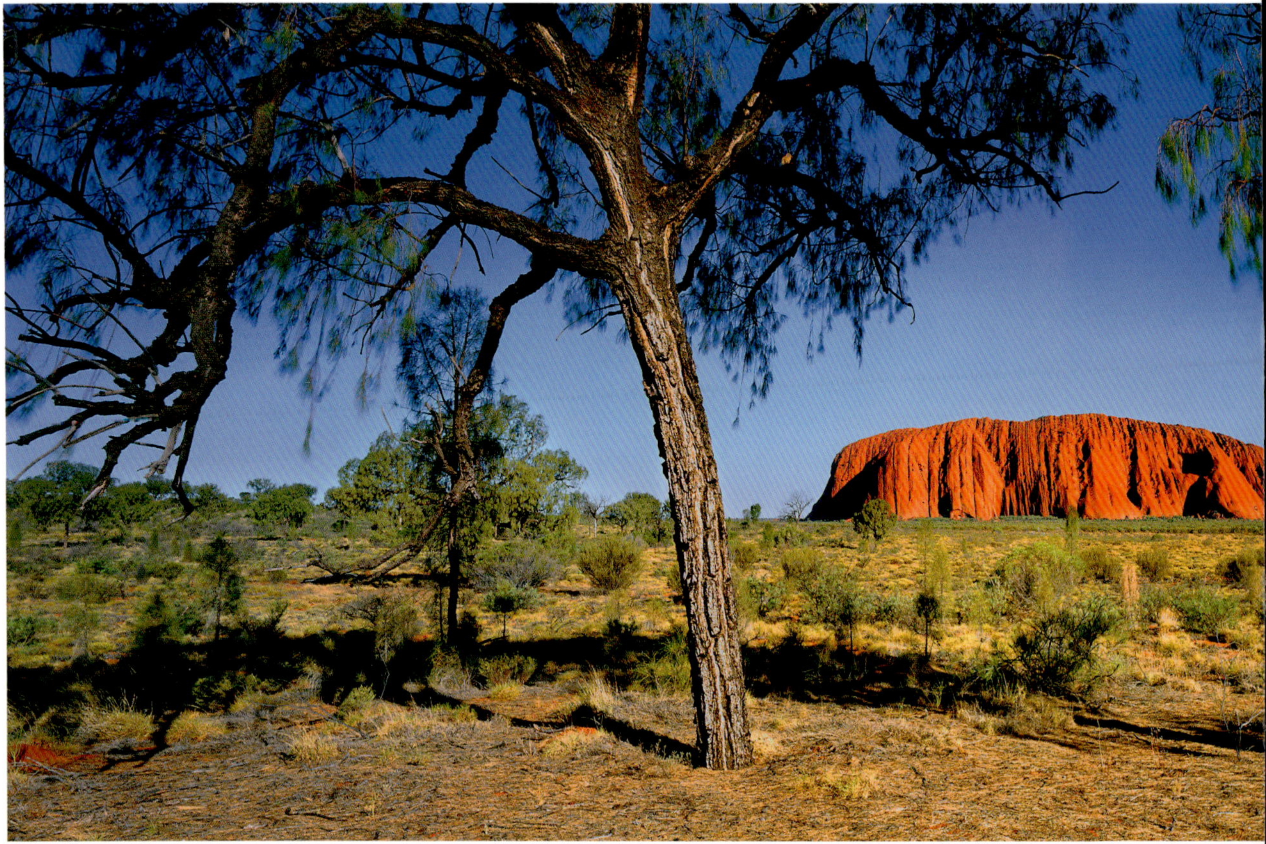

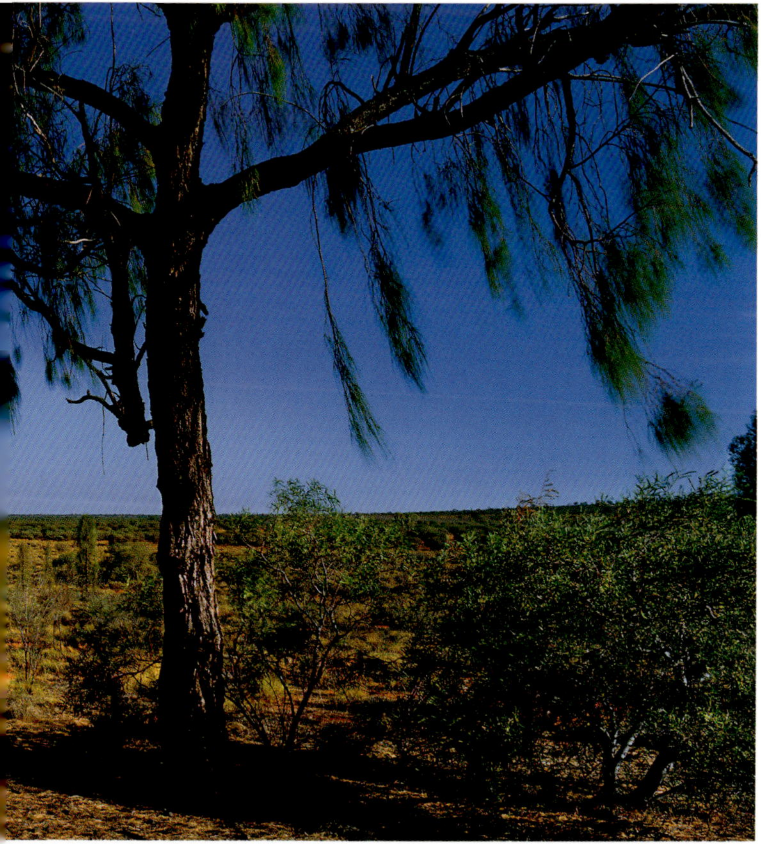

Hope is a foundation from which dreams can be launched.

THIS PAGE
Desert Oaks, Uluru, NT

FOLLOWING PAGES
Reach for Life, Russell Falls, Tas

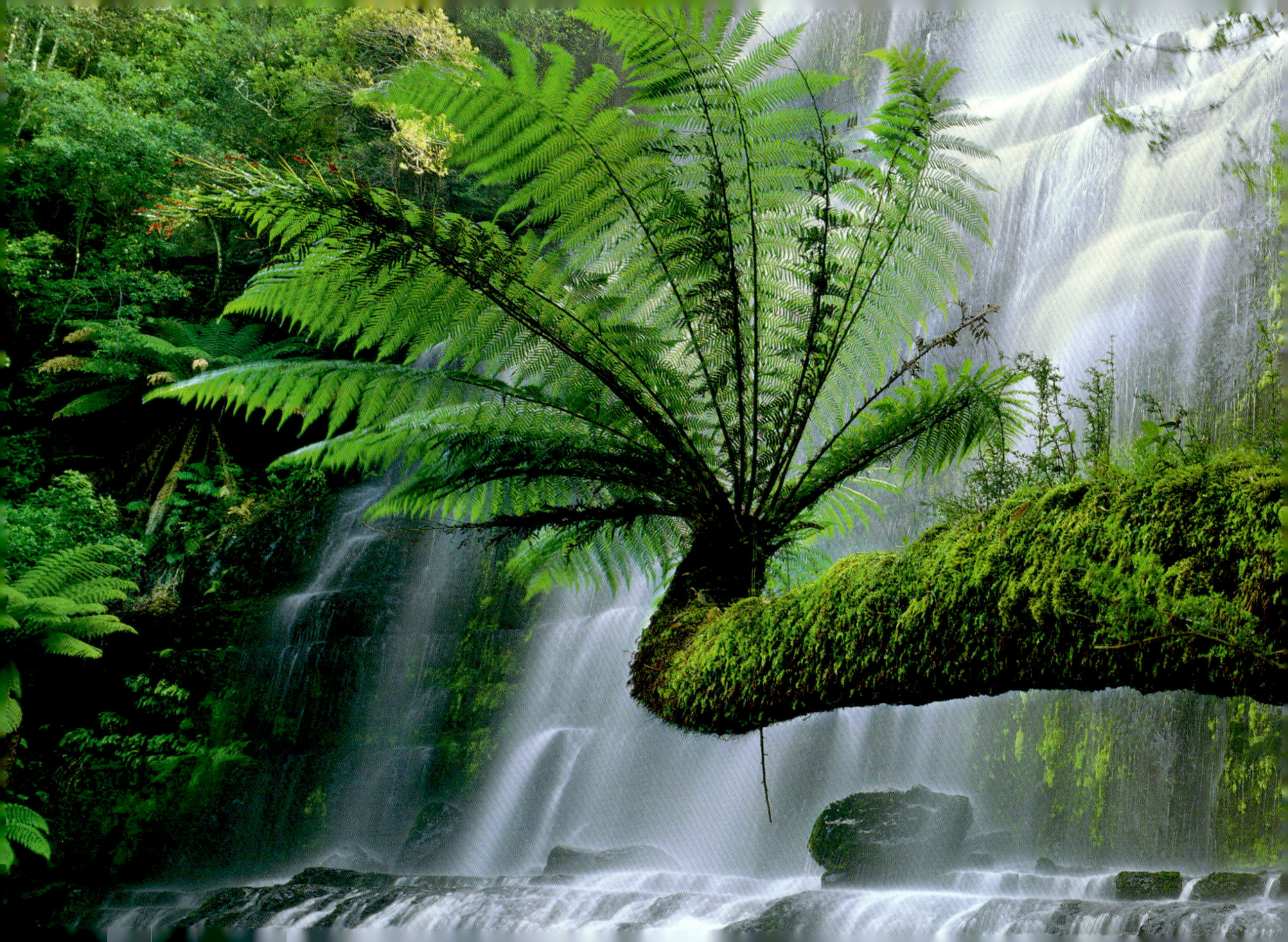

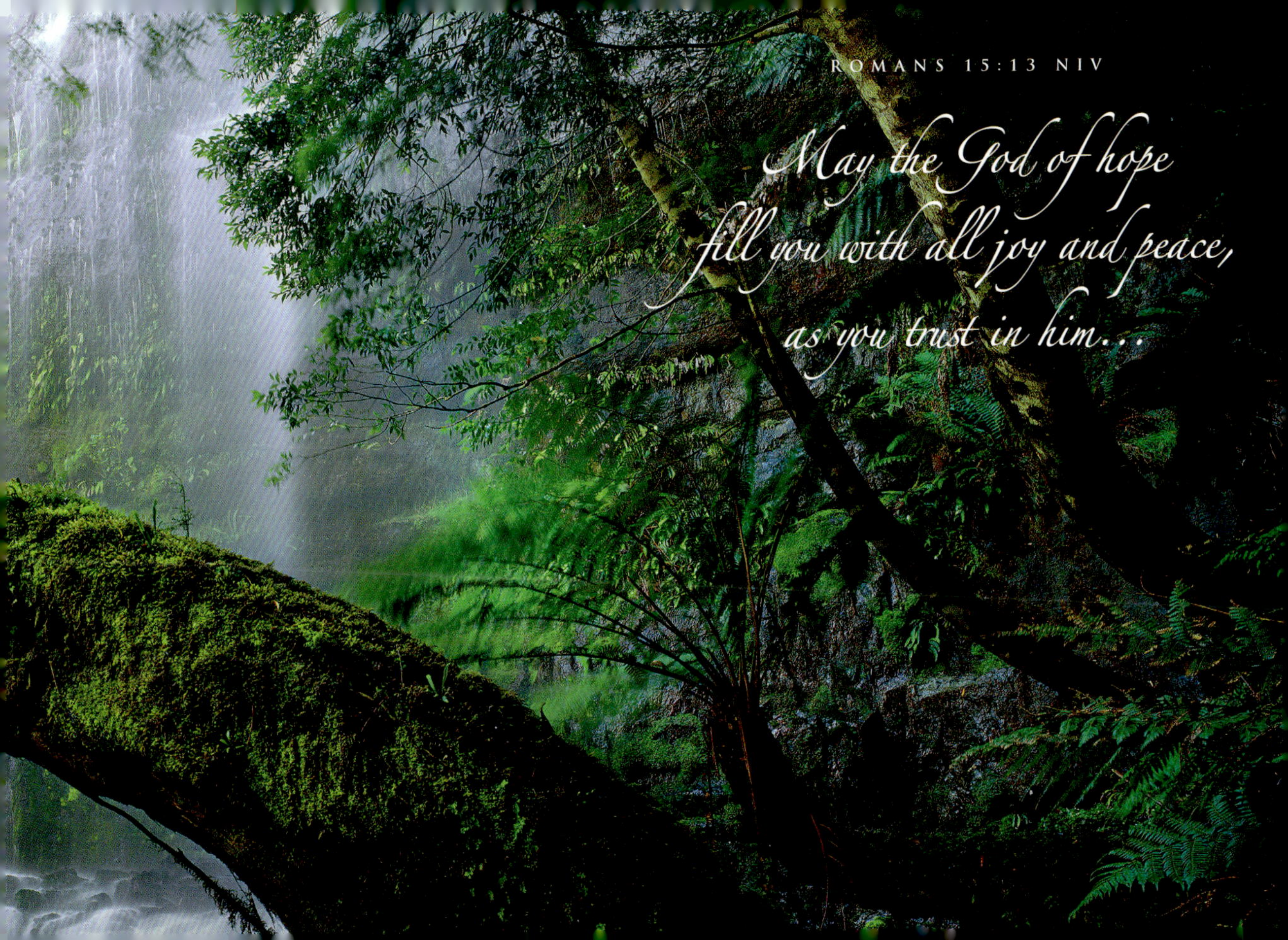
ROMANS 15:13 NIV
May the God of hope
fill you with all joy and peace,
as you trust in him…

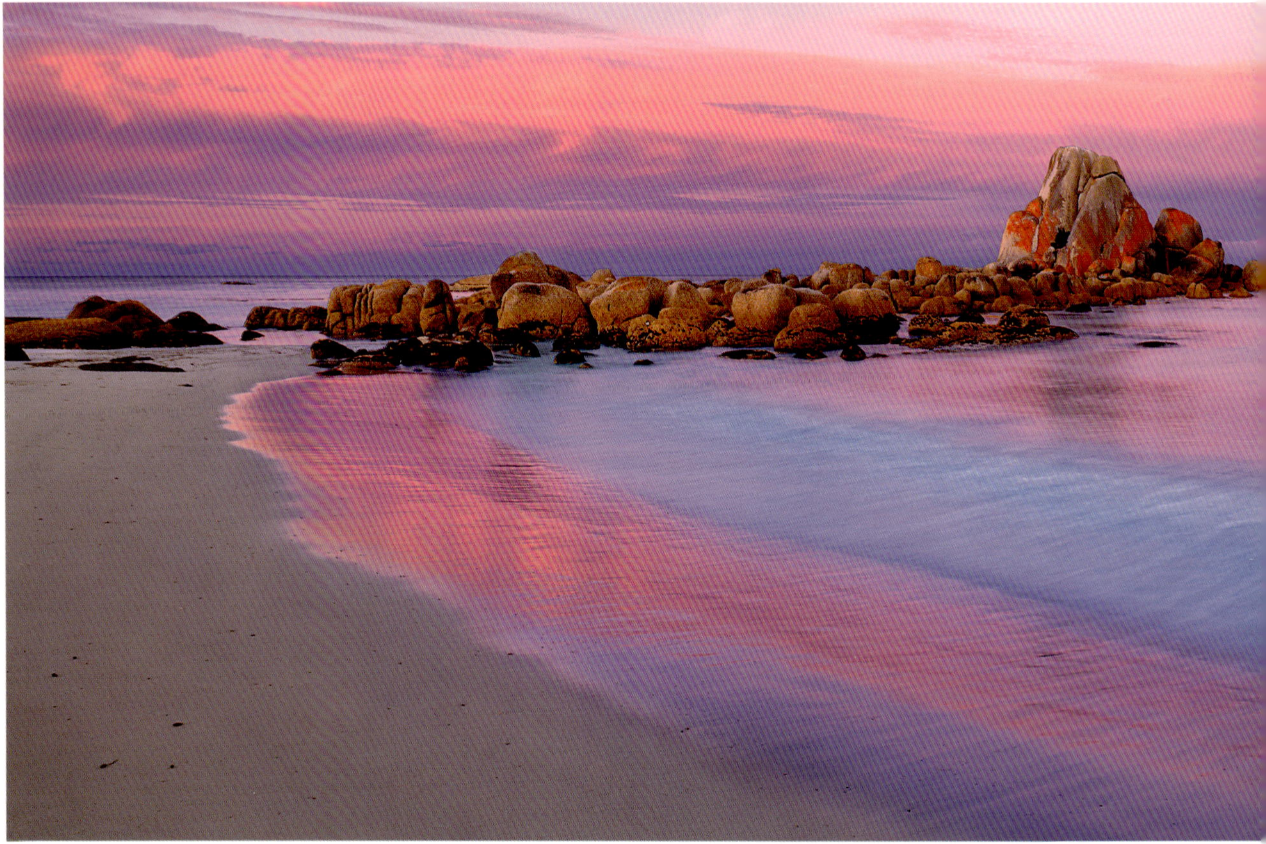

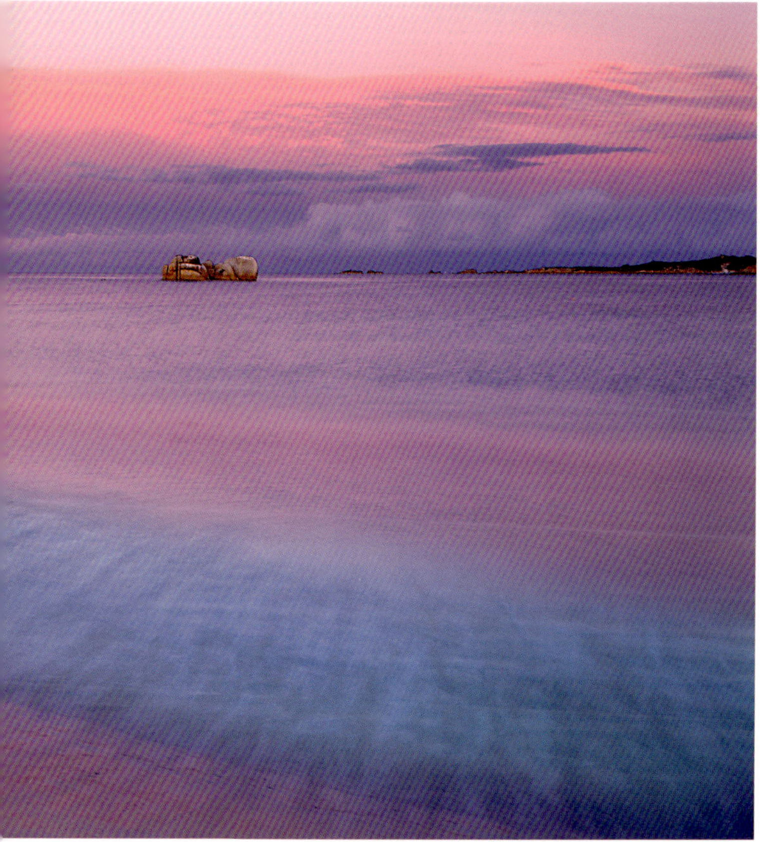

You cannot swim
for new horizons
until you have courage
to lose sight of the shore.

Sunset, Picnic Rocks, Tas

When you feel like hope is lost,
look inside you and be strong.
And you will finally see the truth,
that a hero lies in you.

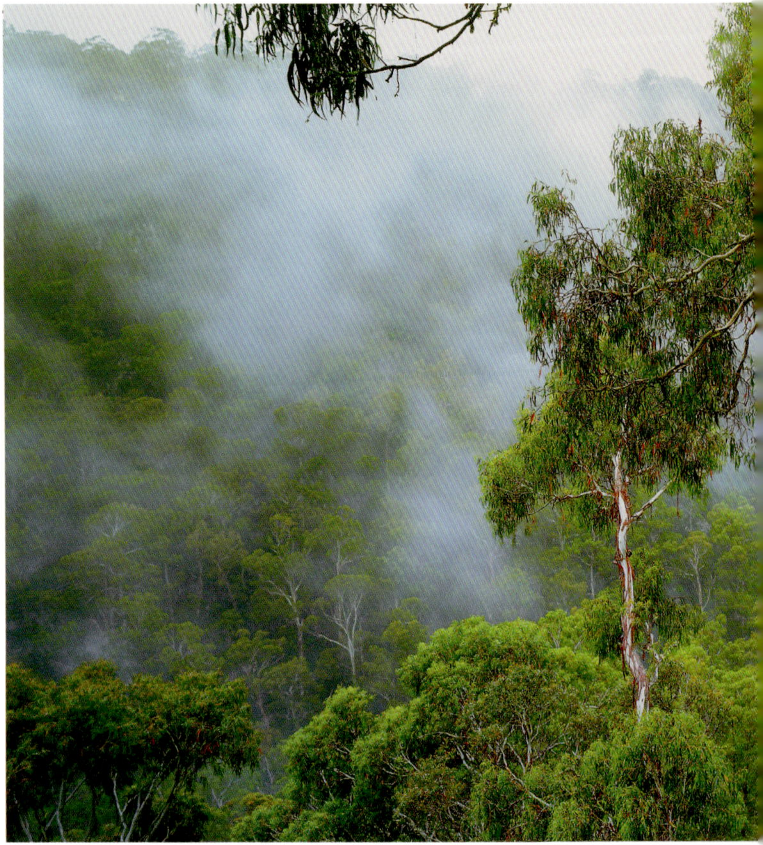

THIS PAGE
Peace in the Valley, Ebor Falls, NSW

FOLLOWING PAGES
Heartland, Haasts Bluff, NT

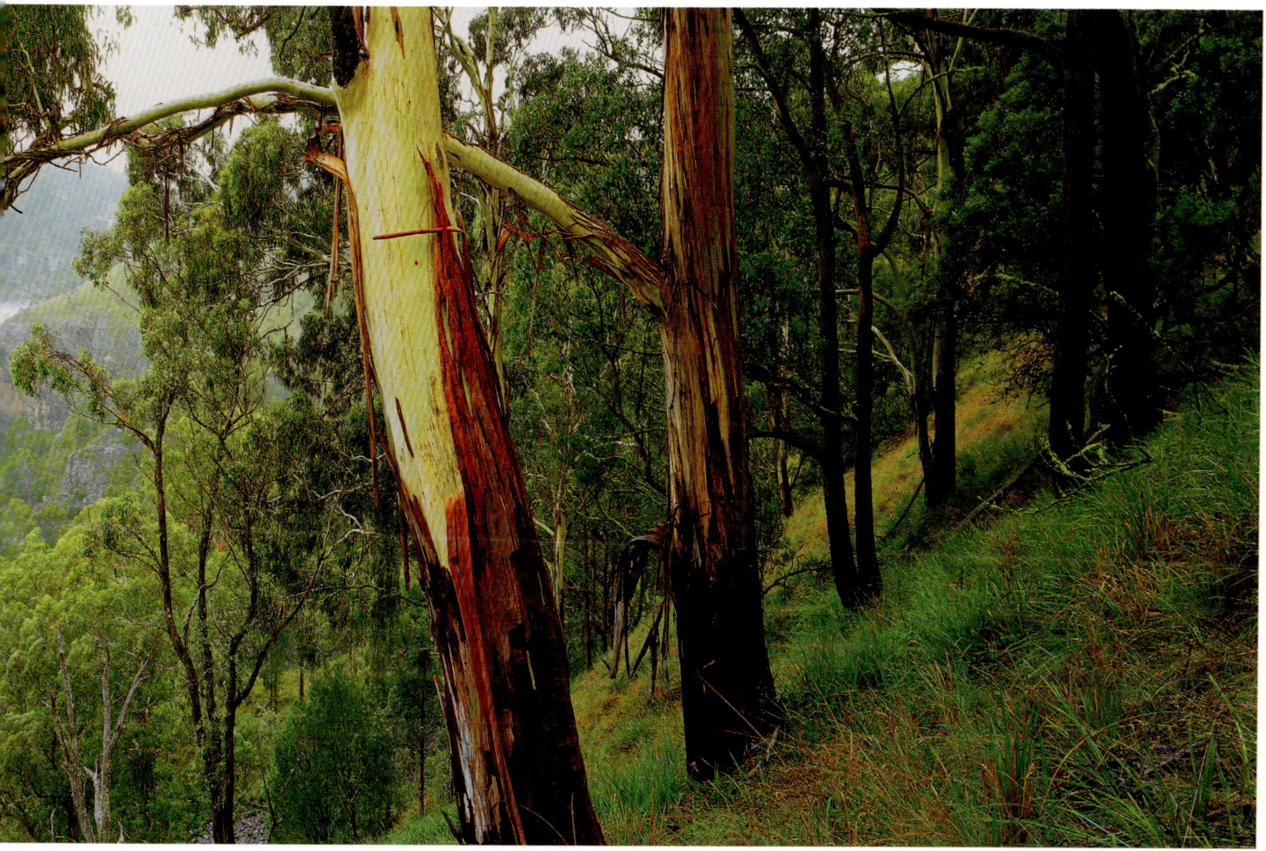

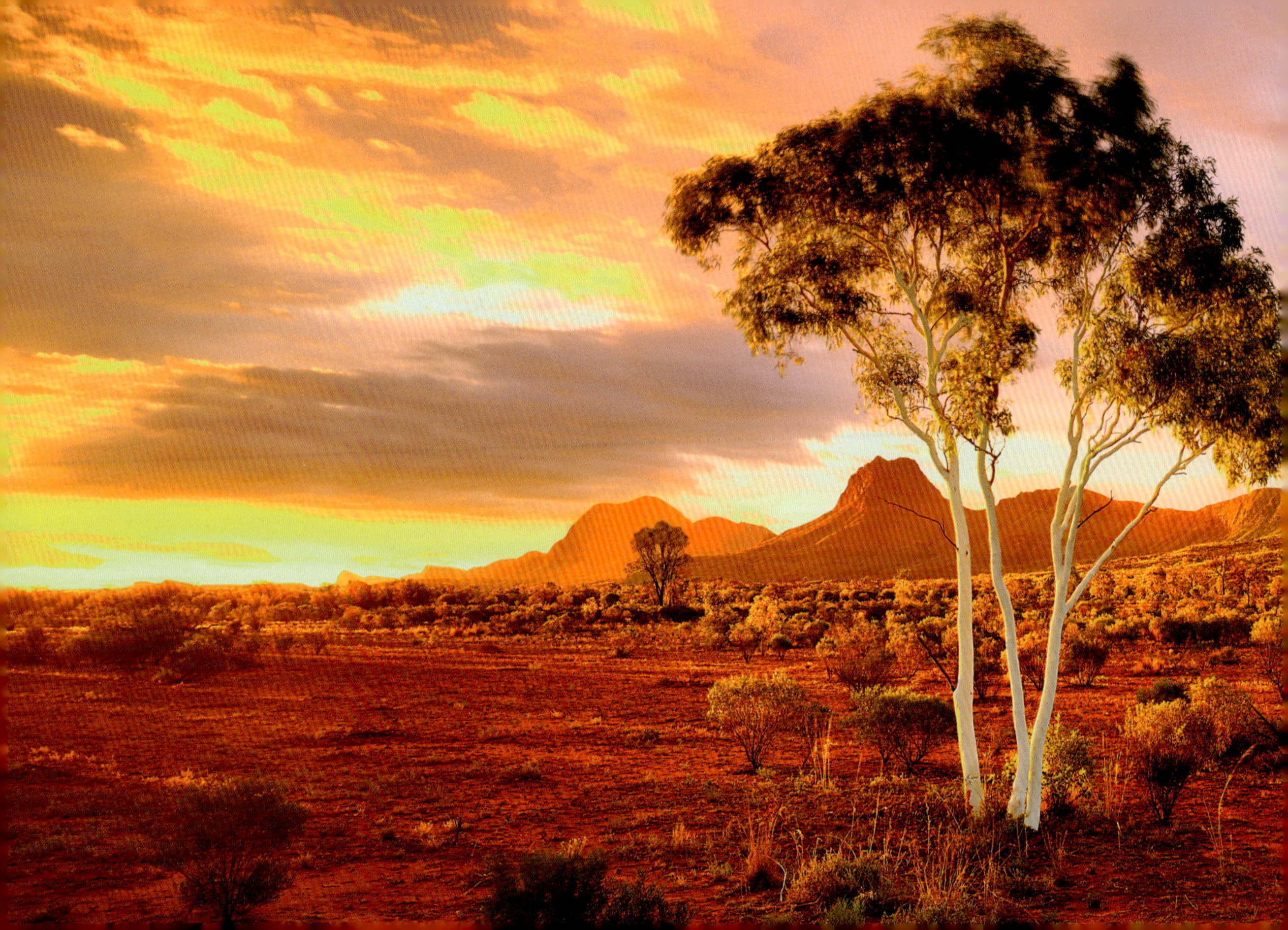

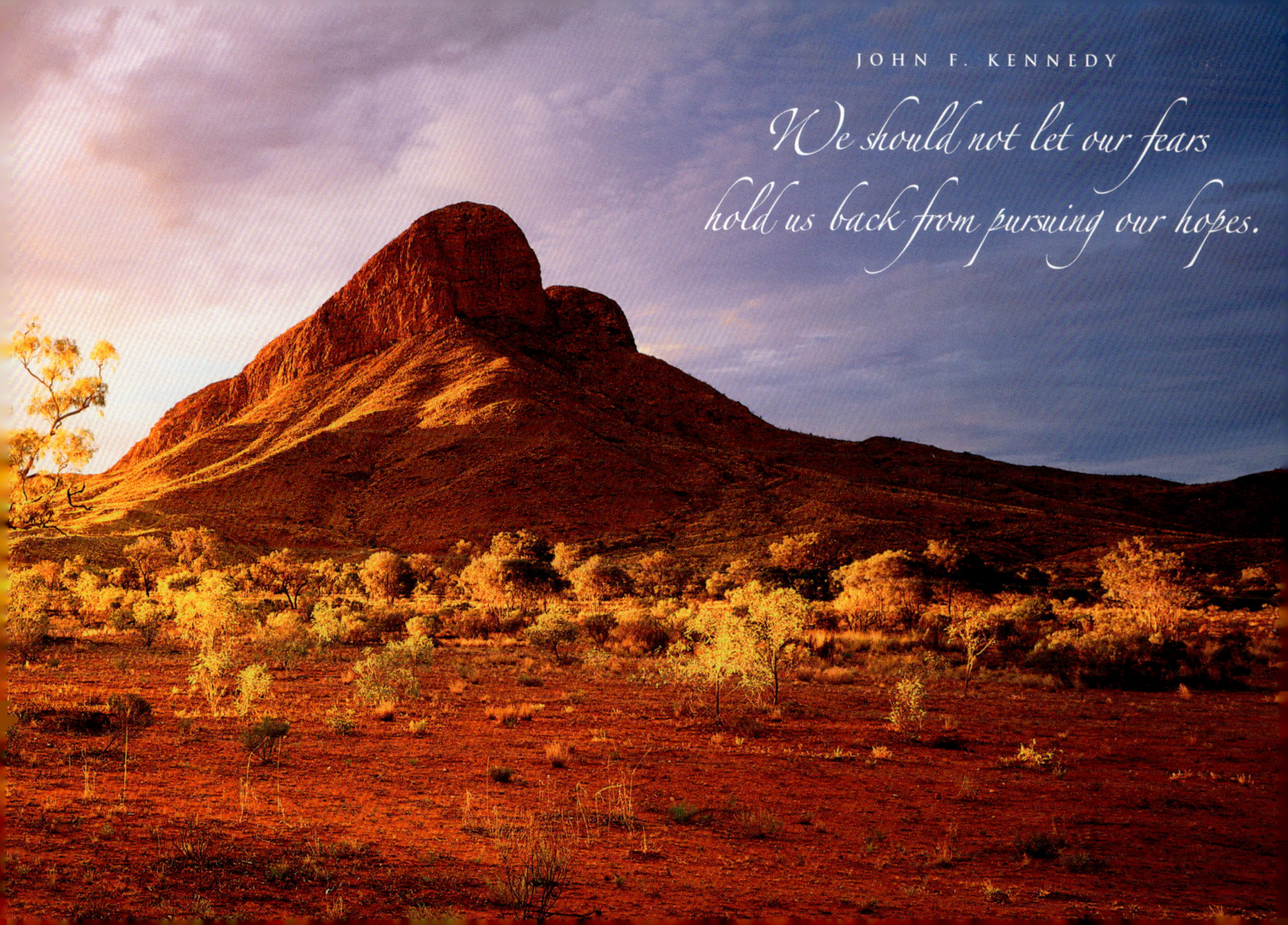
JOHN F. KENNEDY
We should not let our fears
hold us back from pursuing our hopes.

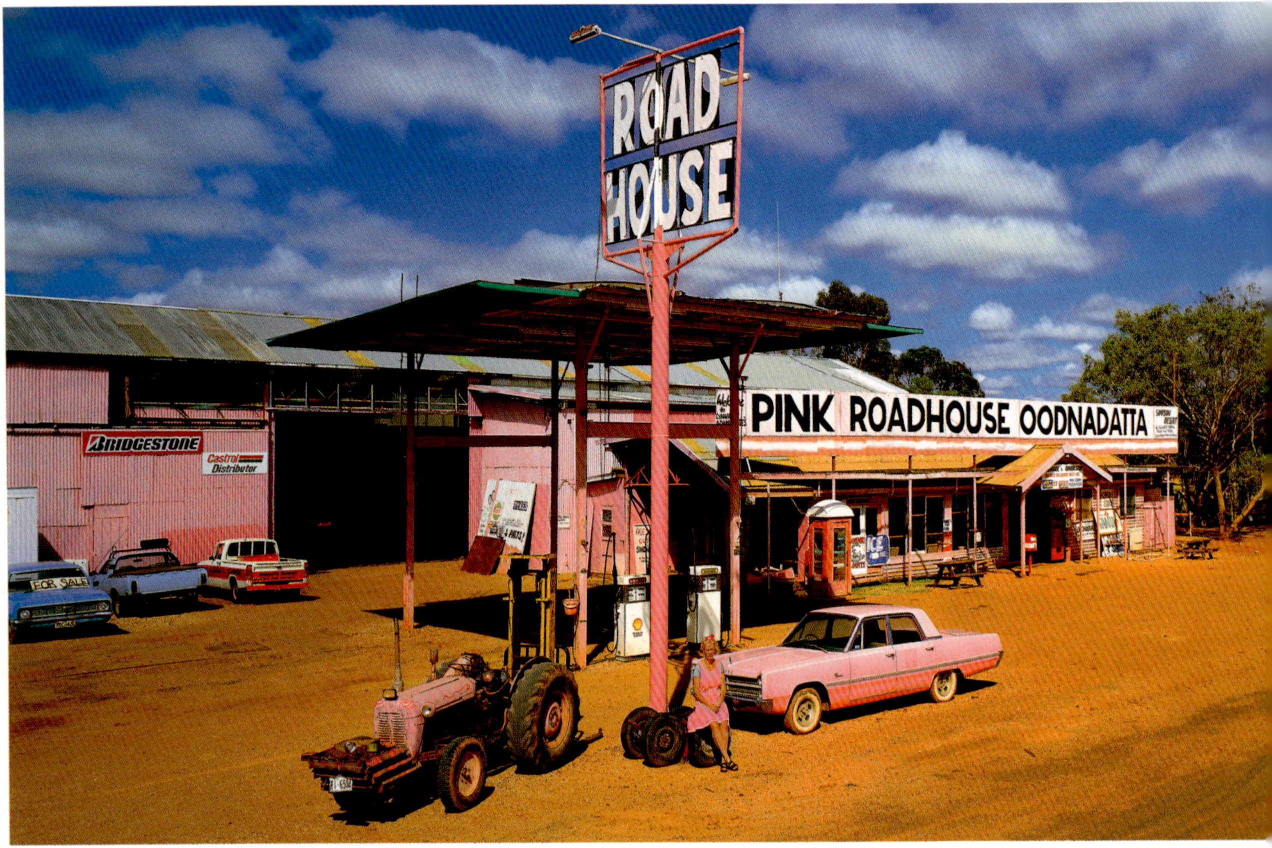
ROAD HOUSE
PINK ROADHOUSE OODNADATTA
BRIDGESTONE
Castrol Distributor
FOR SALE

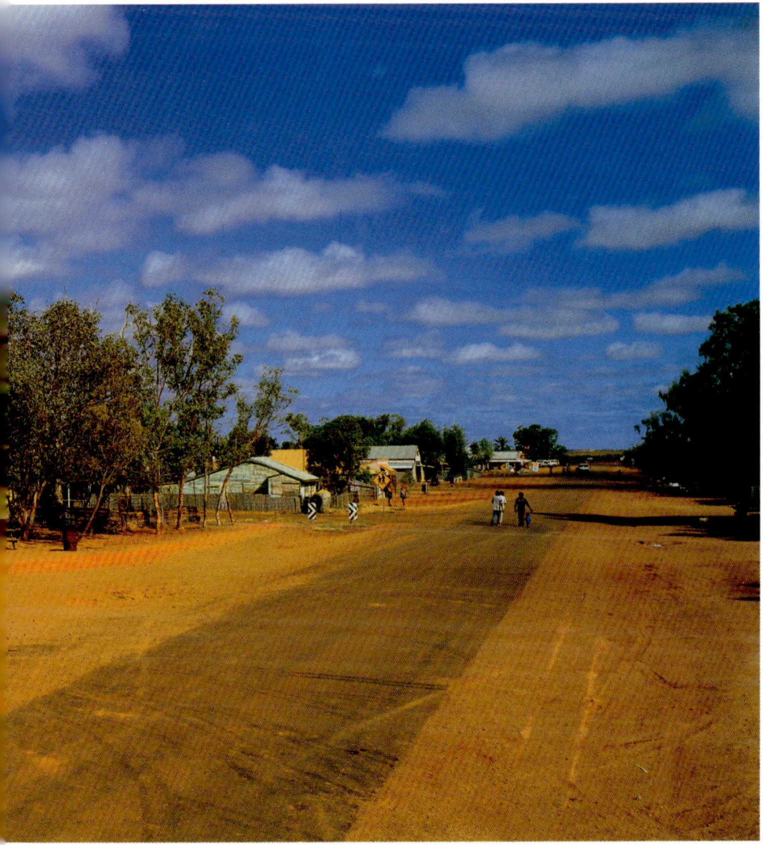

May your choices
reflect your hopes,
not your fears.

The Pink Roadhouse, Oodnadatta, SA

Most of the important things
in the world have been accomplished
by people who have kept on trying
when there seemed to be no hope at all.

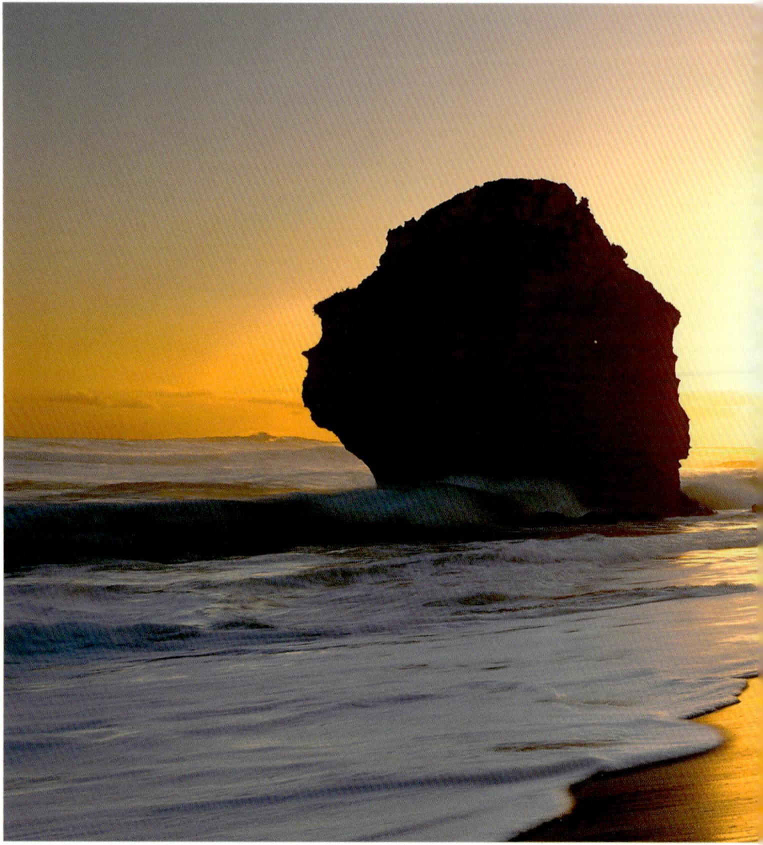

THIS PAGE
Face of the Ages, The Twelve Apostles, Vic

FOLLOWING PAGES
Eternal Wonder, King George Falls, WA

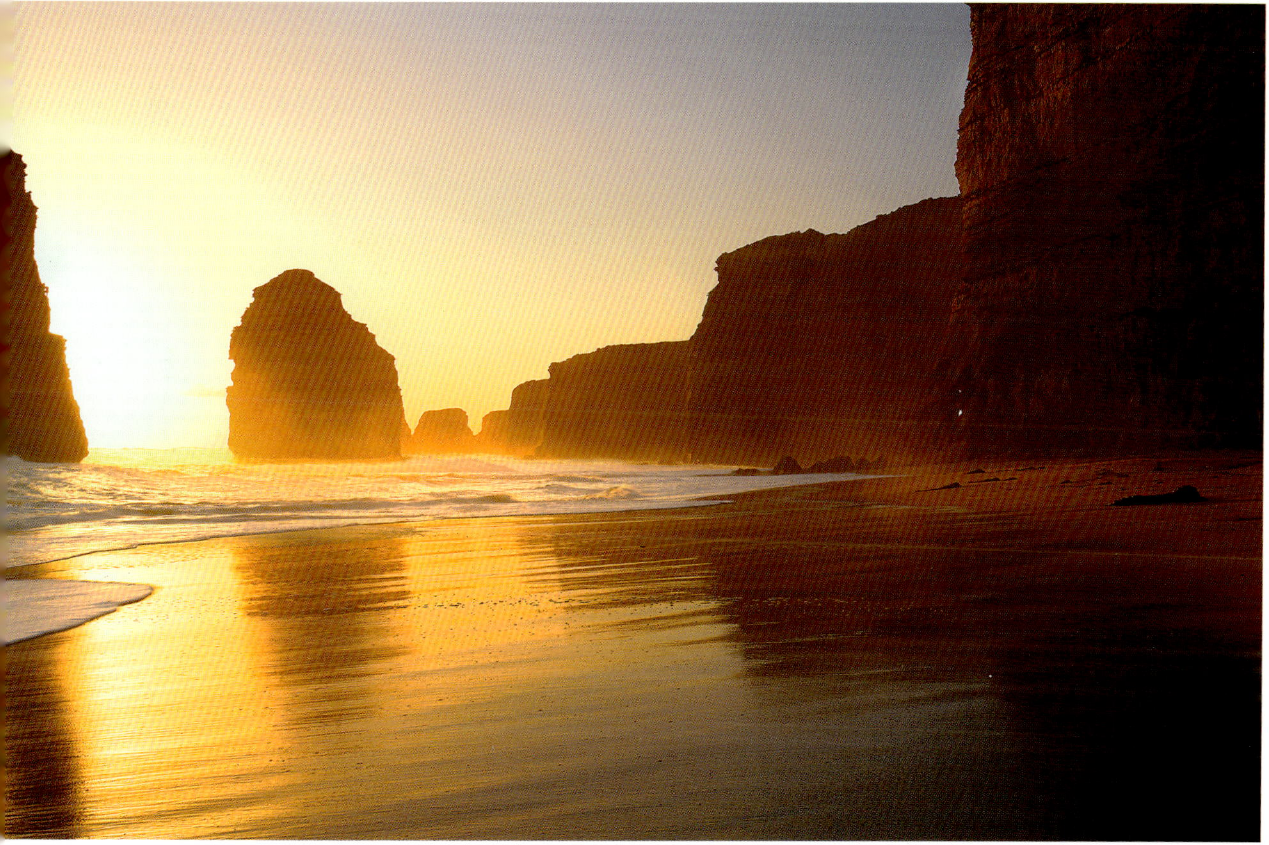

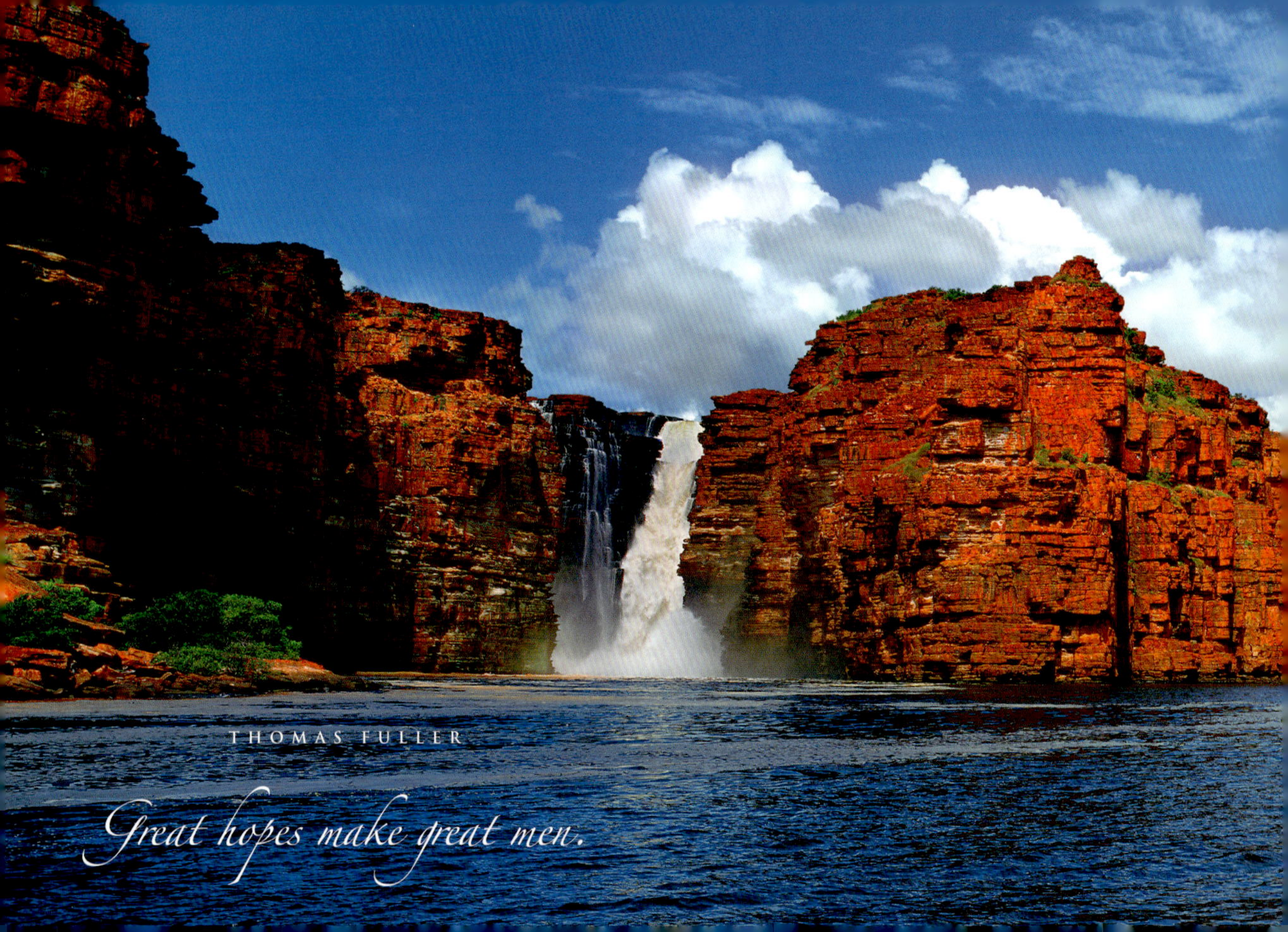

THOMAS FULLER

Great hopes make great men.

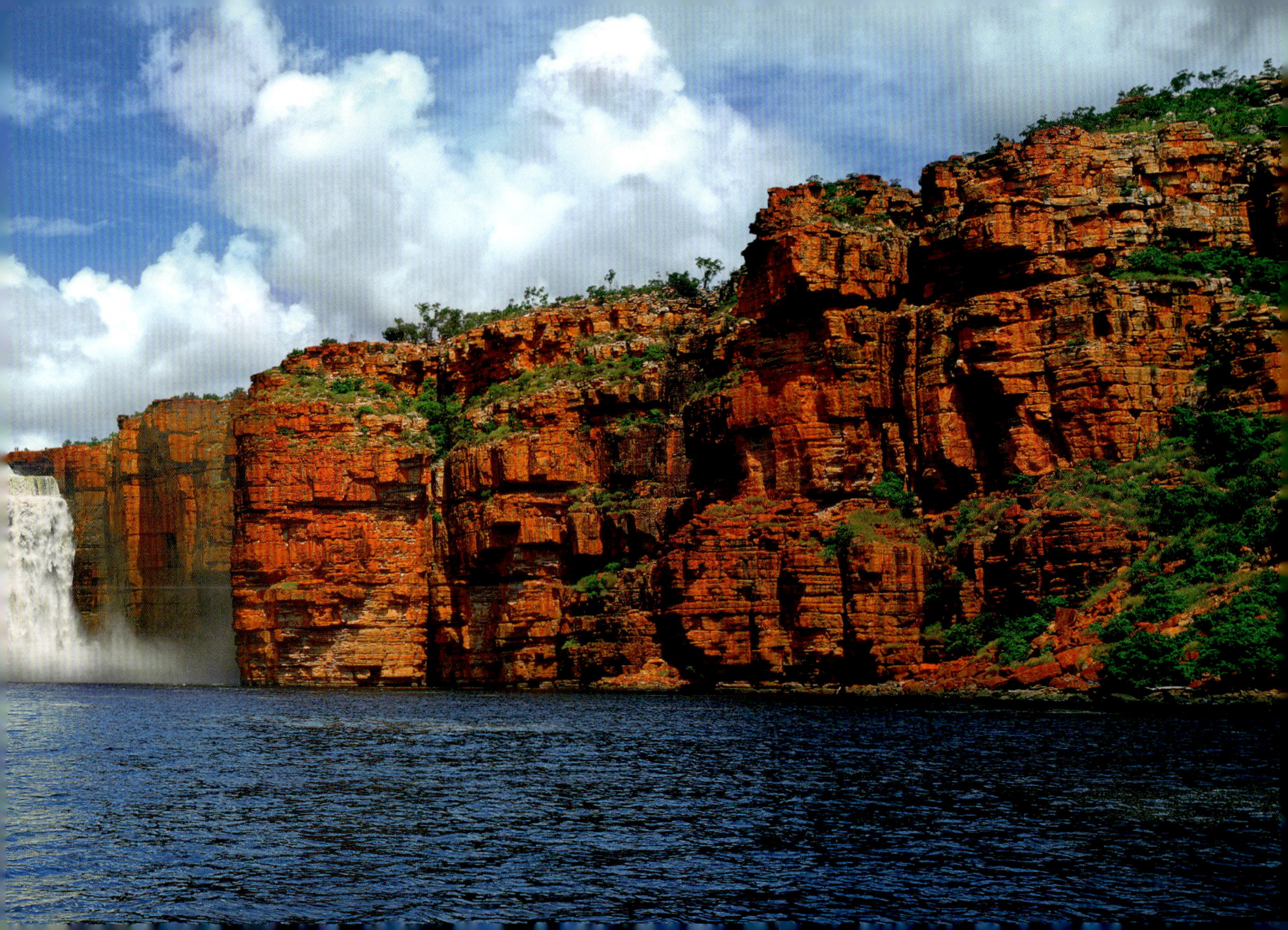

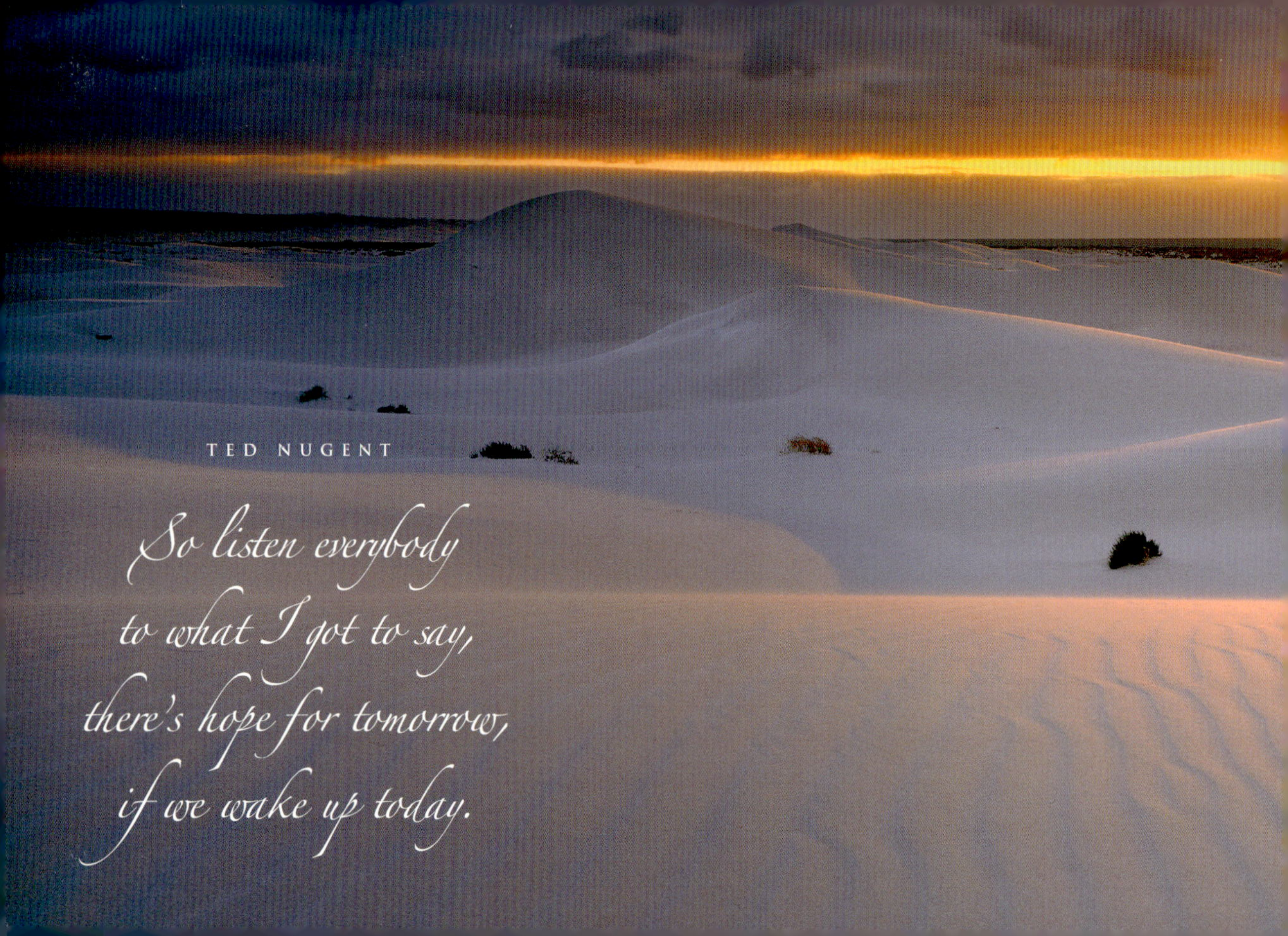

TED NUGENT

So listen everybody
to what I got to say,
there's hope for tomorrow,
if we wake up today.

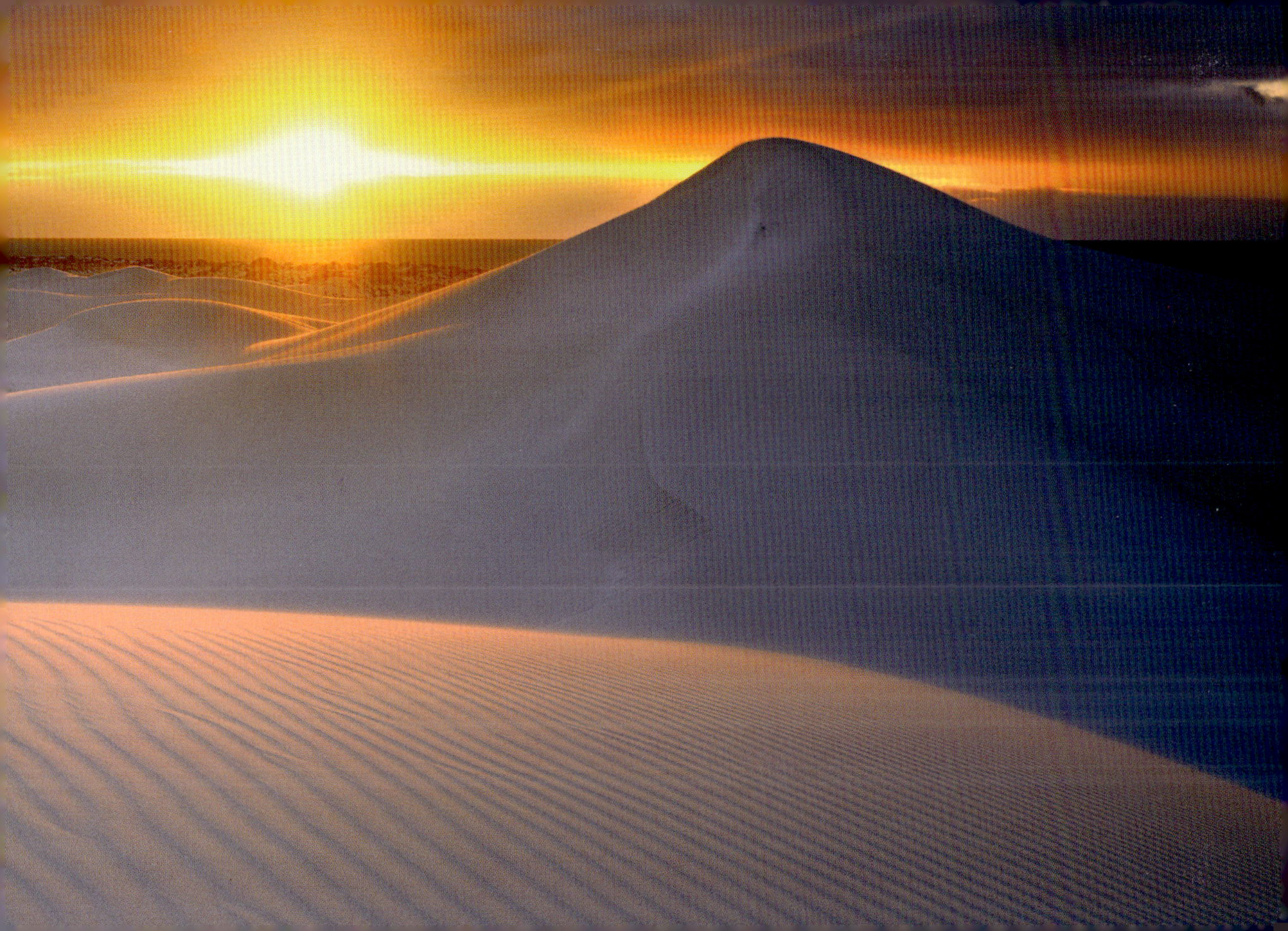

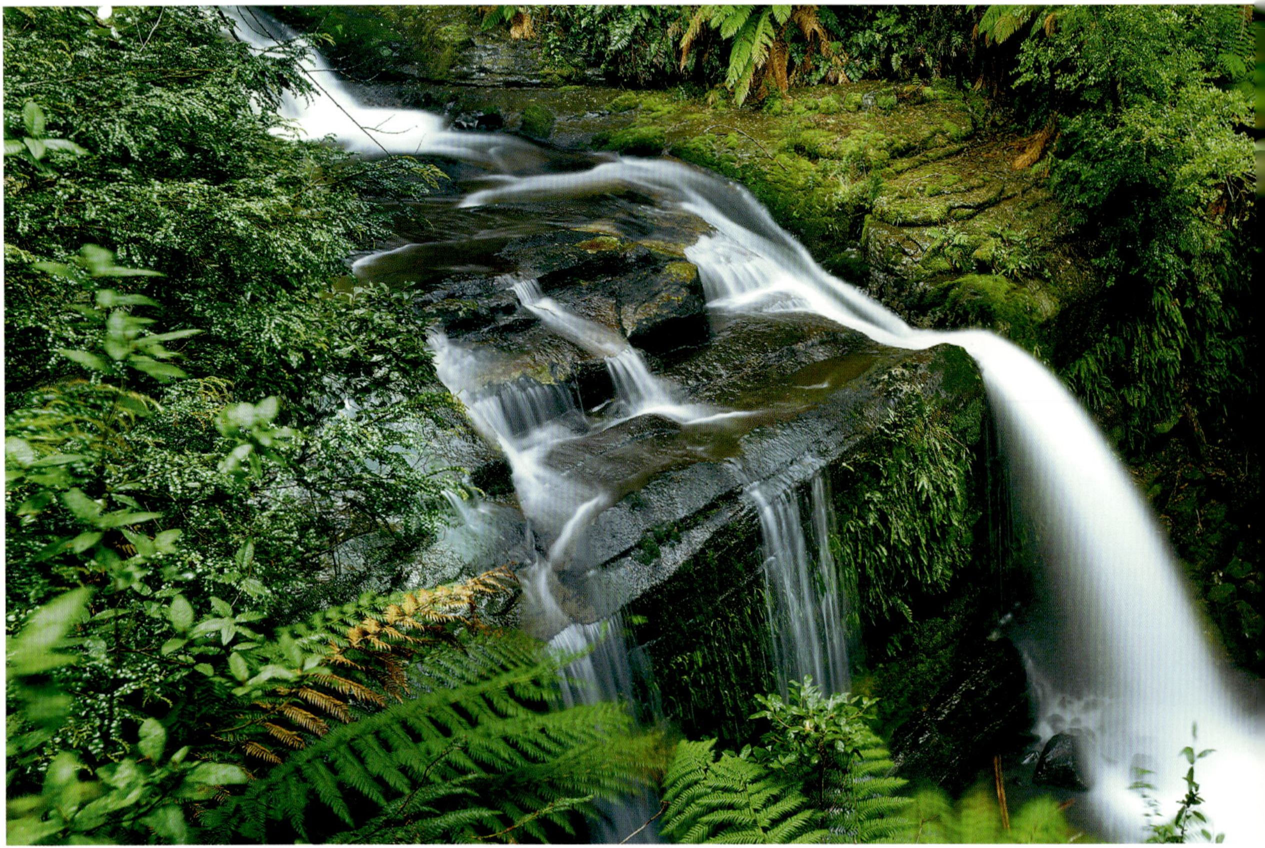

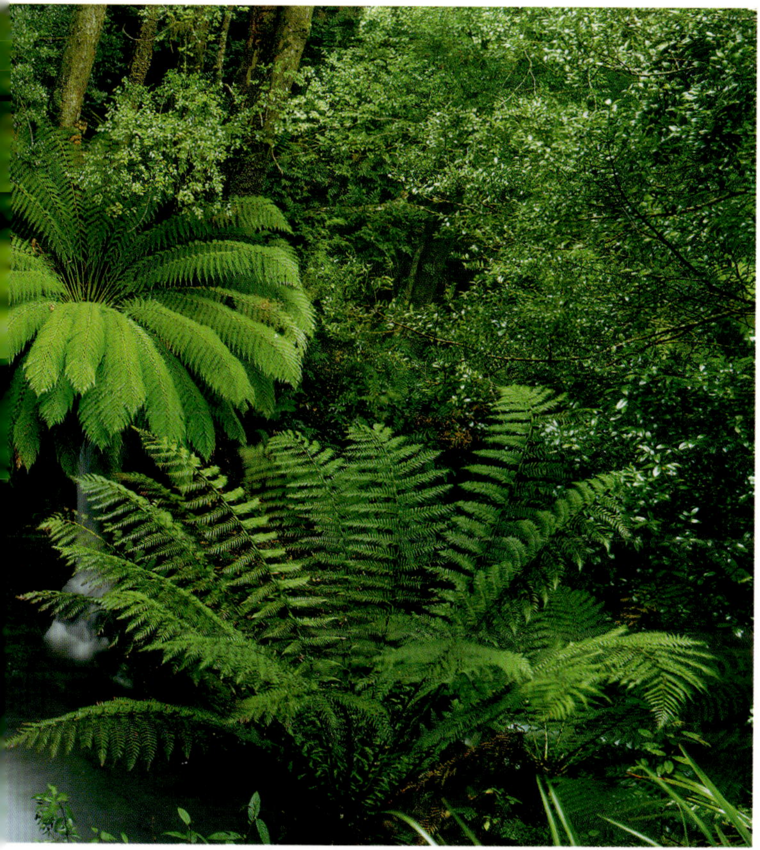

Love recognises no barriers.
It jumps hurdles, leaps fences,
penetrates walls to arrive
at its destination full of hope.

PREVIOUS PAGES
Radiant Dawn, Eucla, WA

THIS PAGE
The Spout, Liffey Falls, Tas

GEORGE WEINBERG

Hope never abandons you;
you abandon it.

THIS PAGE
Ormiston Gorge, NT

FOLLOWING PAGES
Imagine, Chilli Beach, Qld

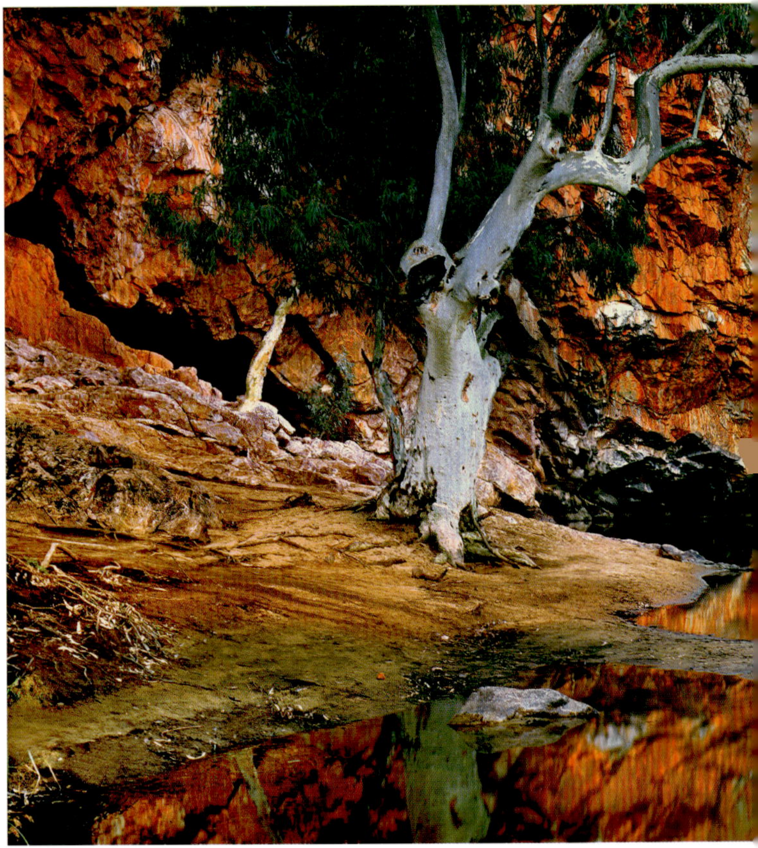

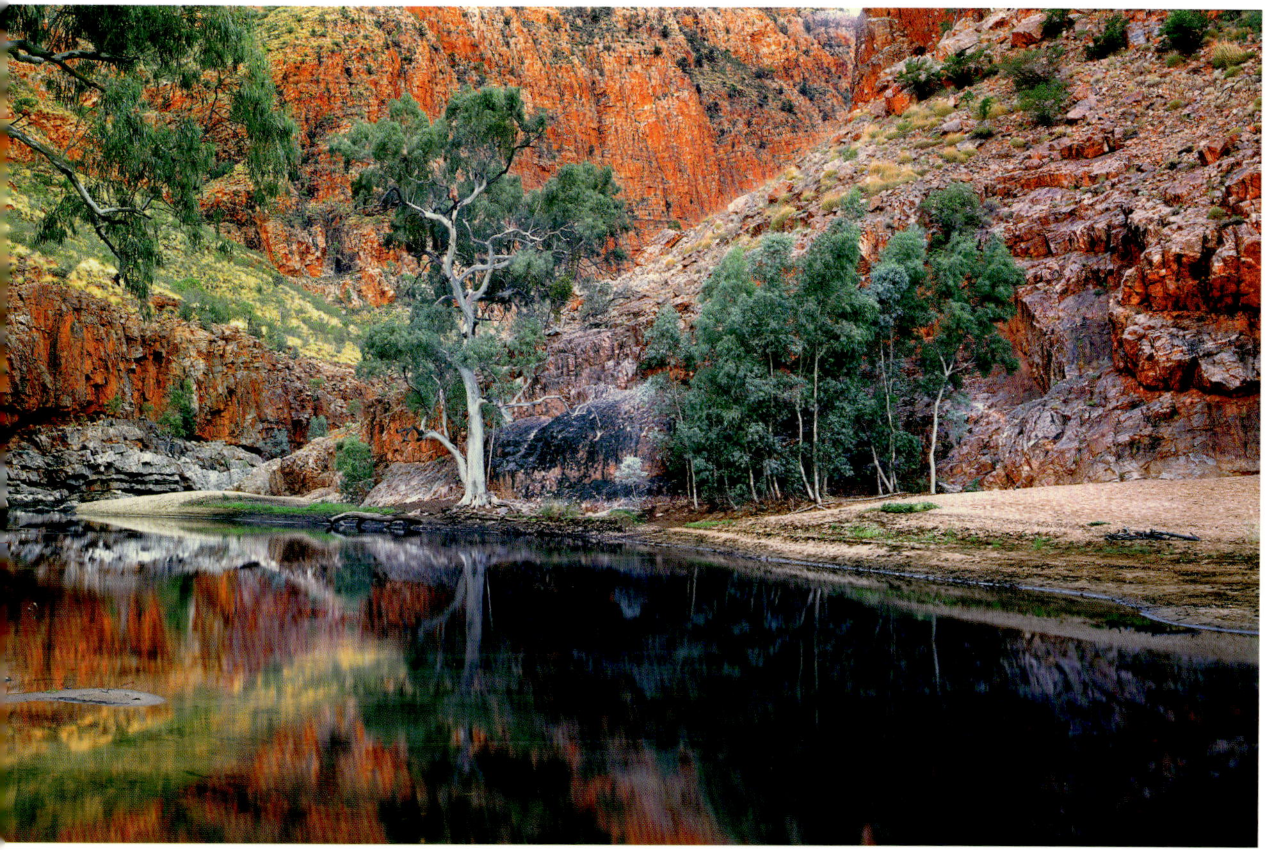

THOMAS CARLYLE

*He who has health, has hope;
and he who has hope, has everything.*

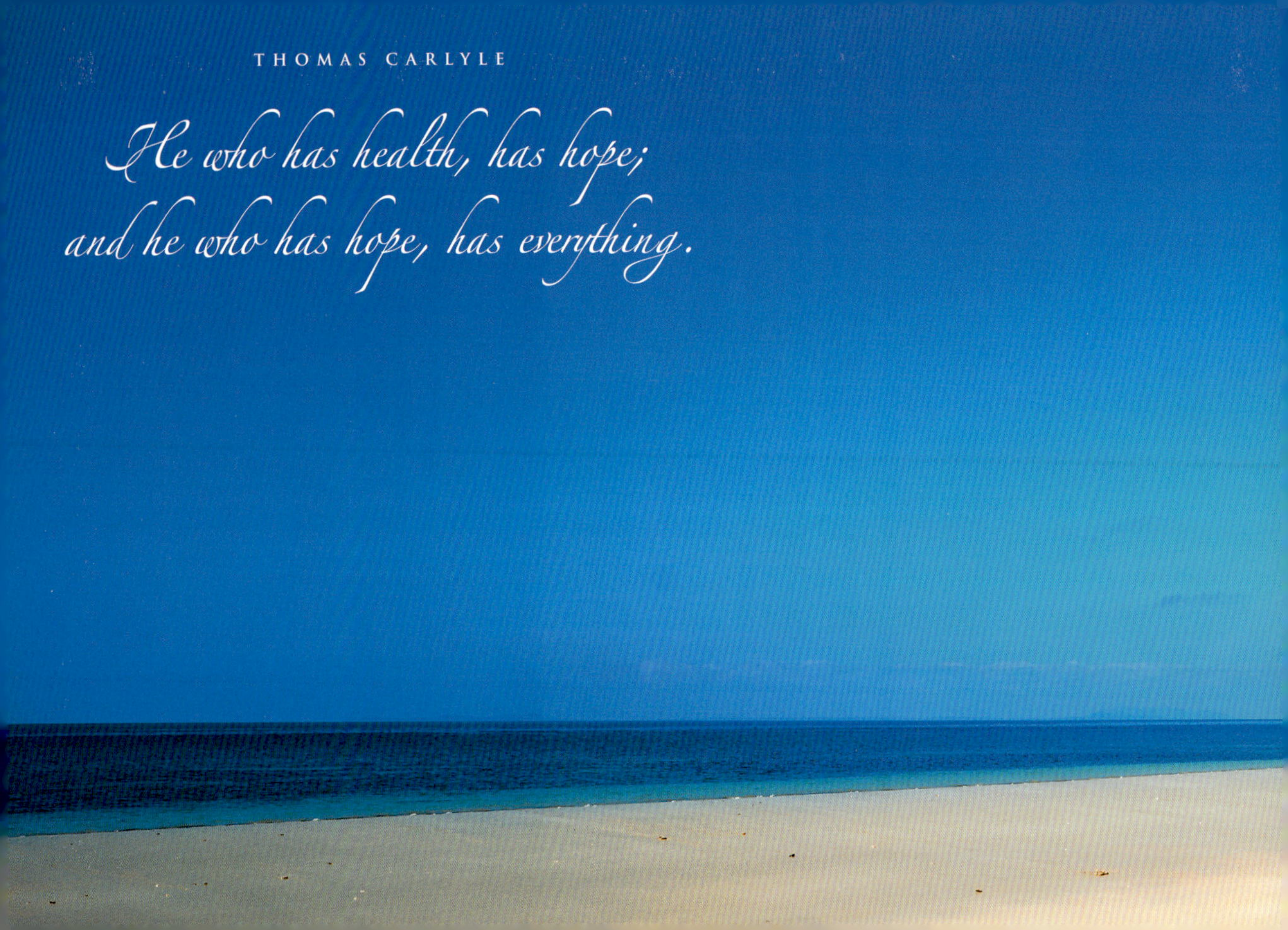

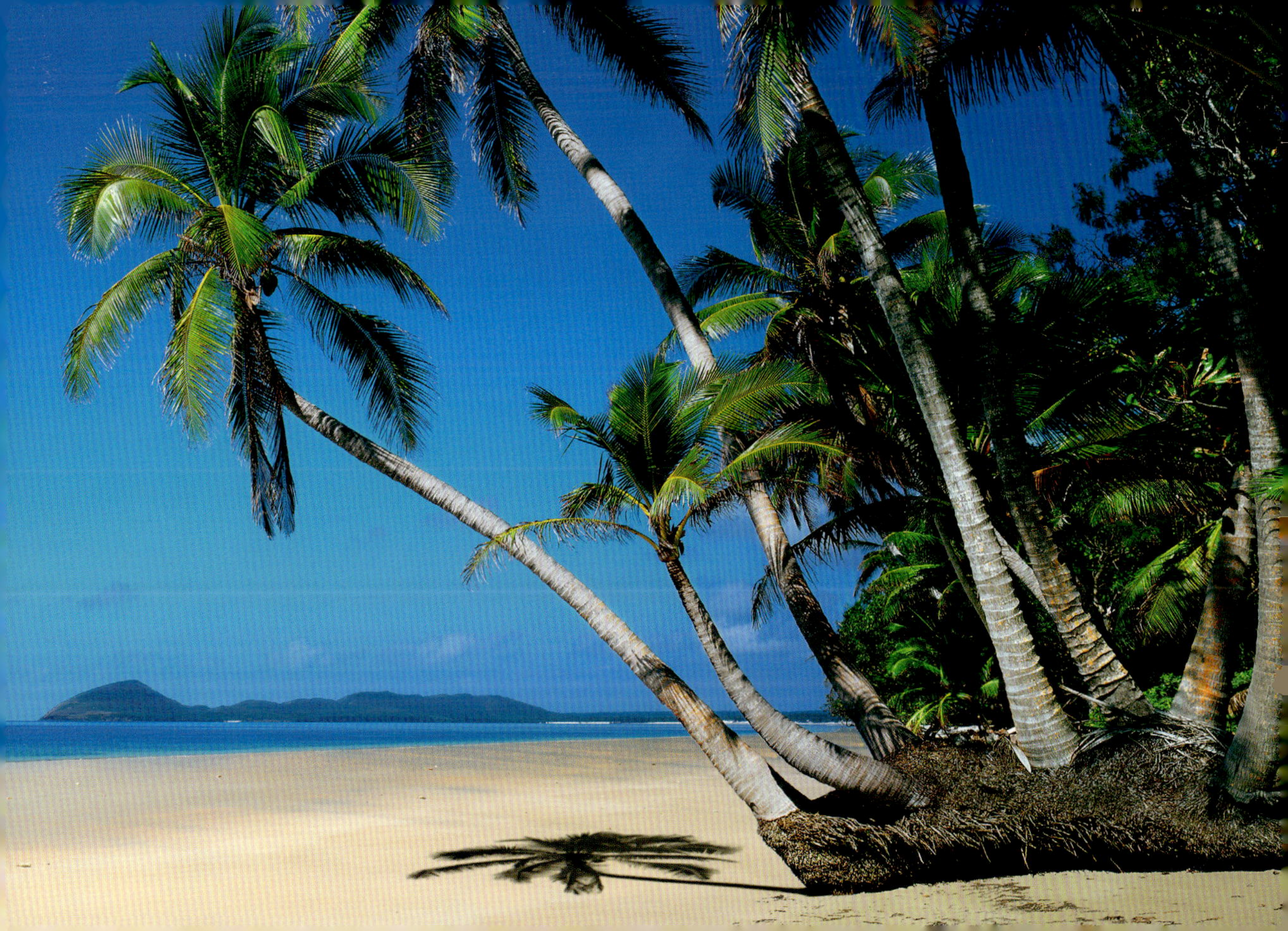

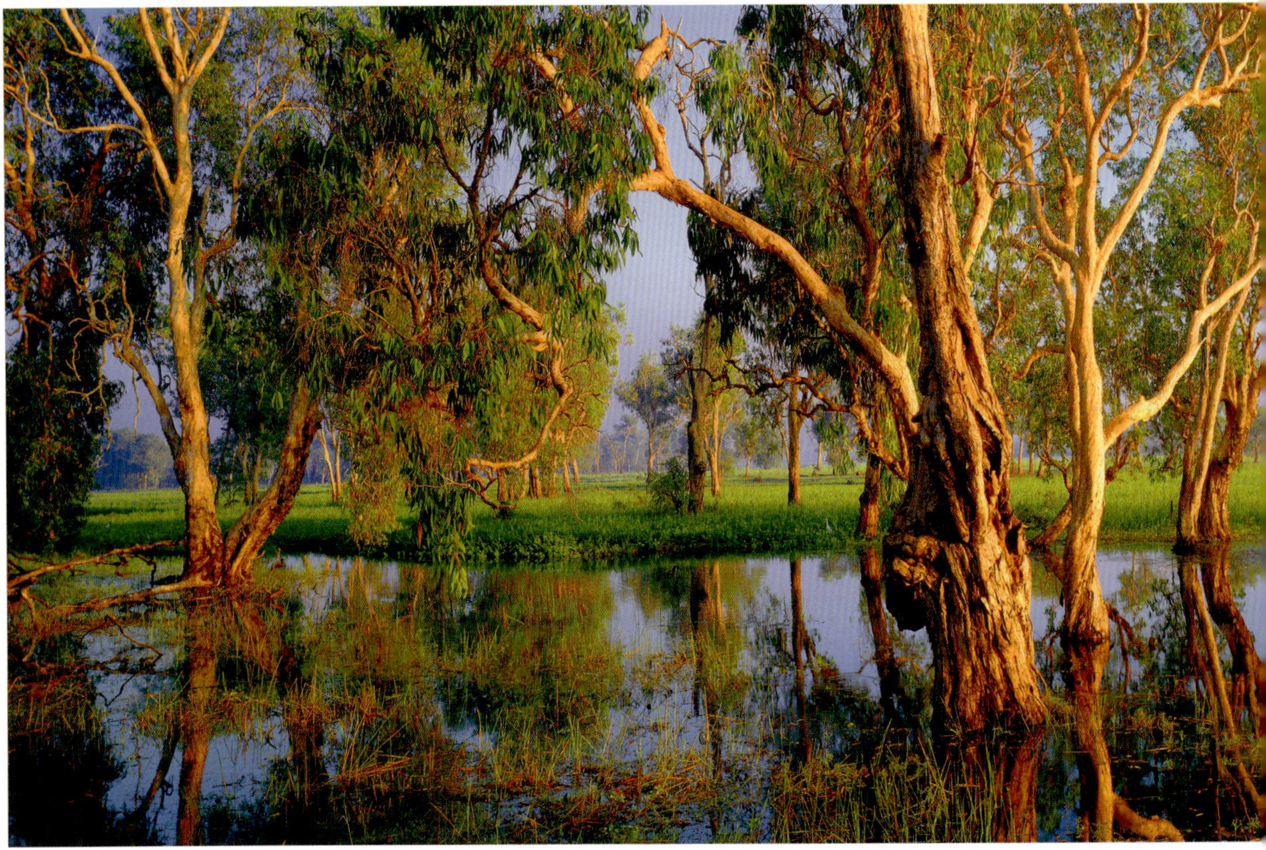

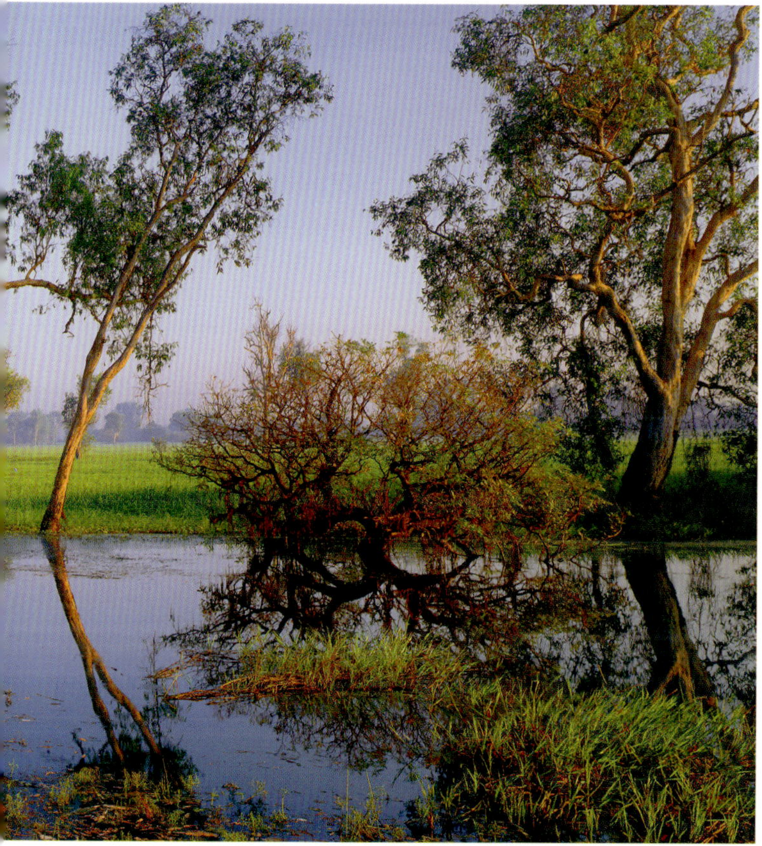

Hey you, don't tell me
there's no hope at all,
together we stand,
divided we fall.

Kakadu Dreaming, Kakadu National Park, NT

Hope is like the sun, which,
as we journey toward it,
casts the shadow of our burden
behind us.

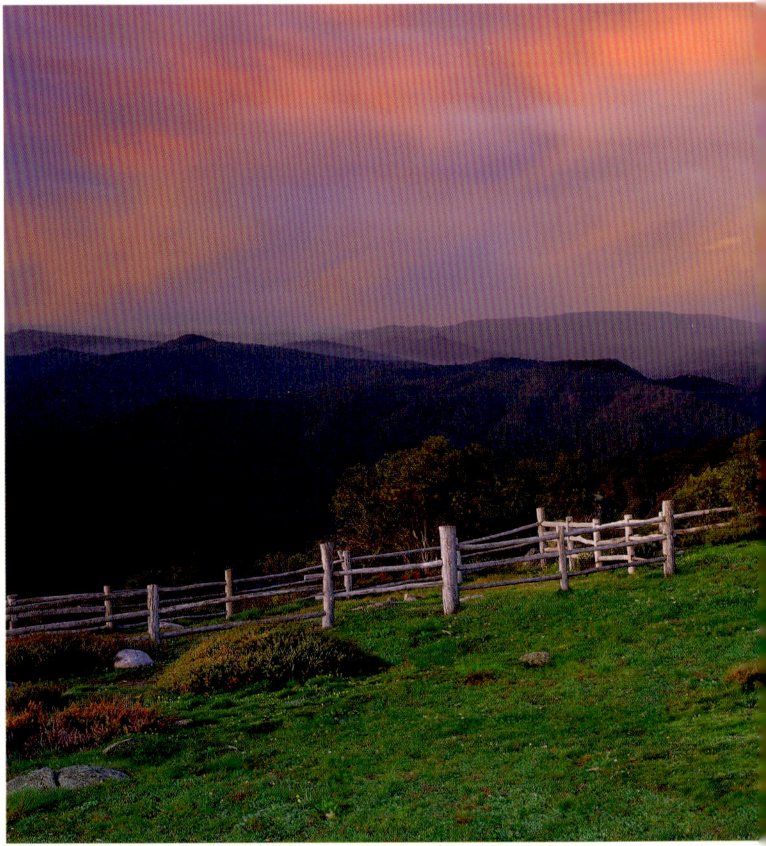

THIS PAGE
Dreams of Yesterday, Craig's Hut, Vic

FOLLOWING PAGES
Heavenly Shroud, Dorrigo National Park, NSW

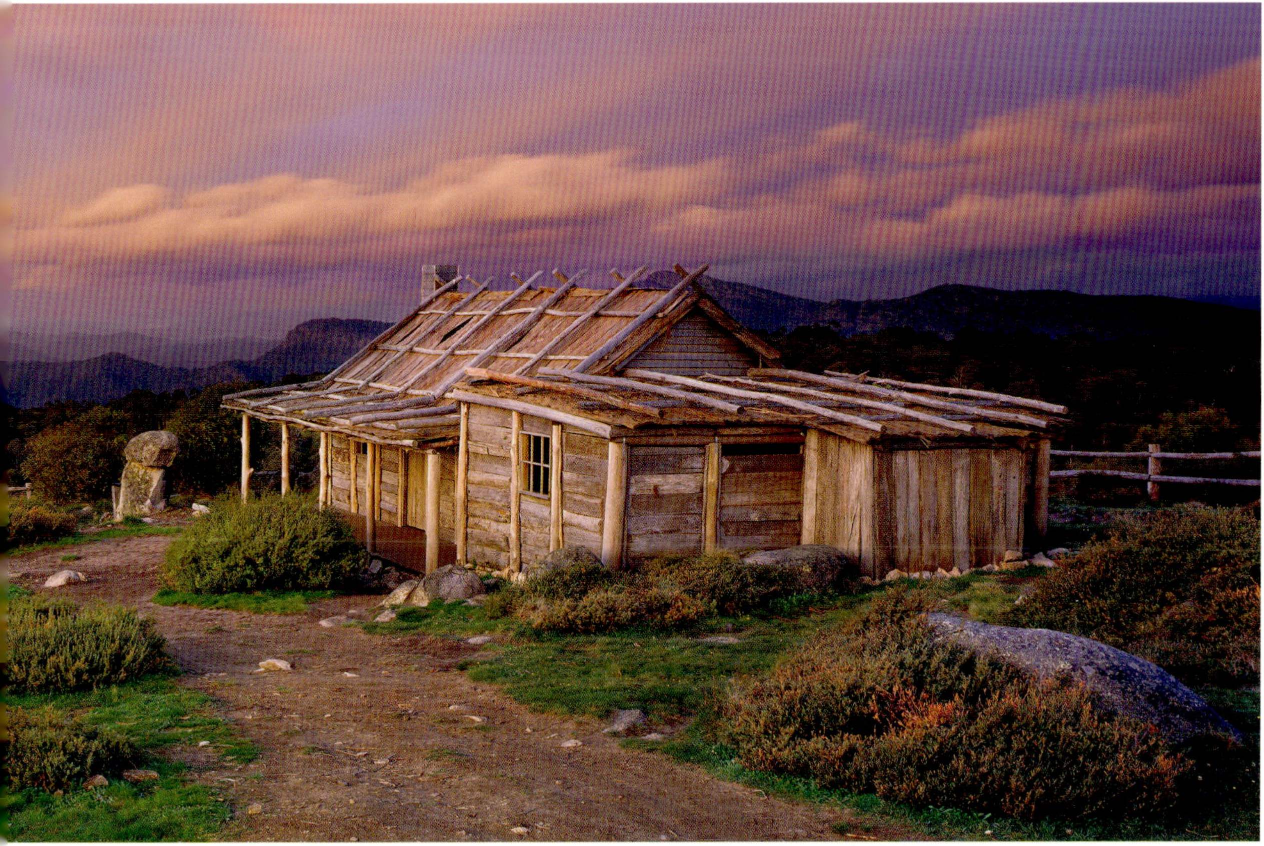

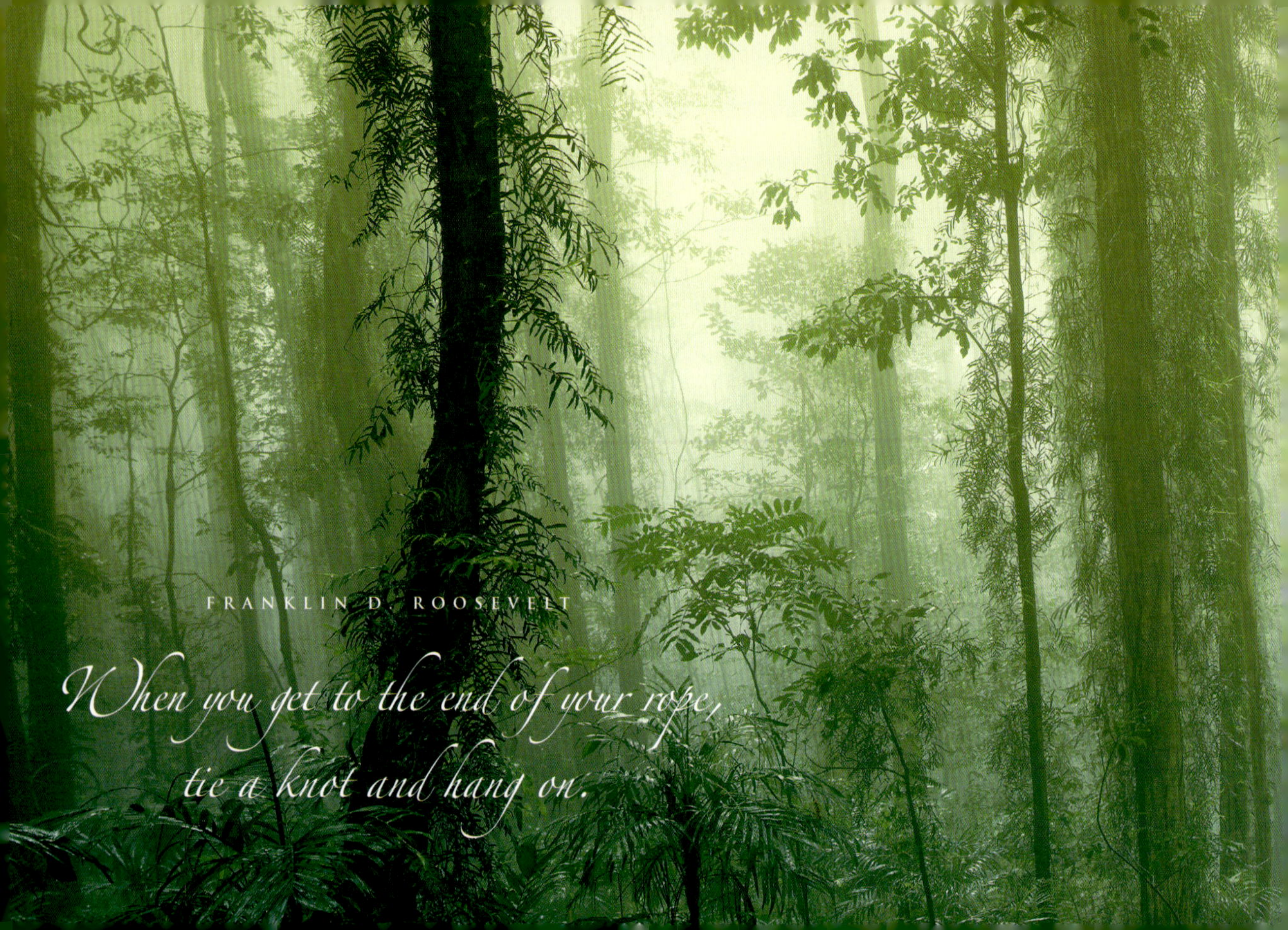
FRANKLIN D. ROOSEVELT
When you get to the end of your rope,
tie a knot and hang on.

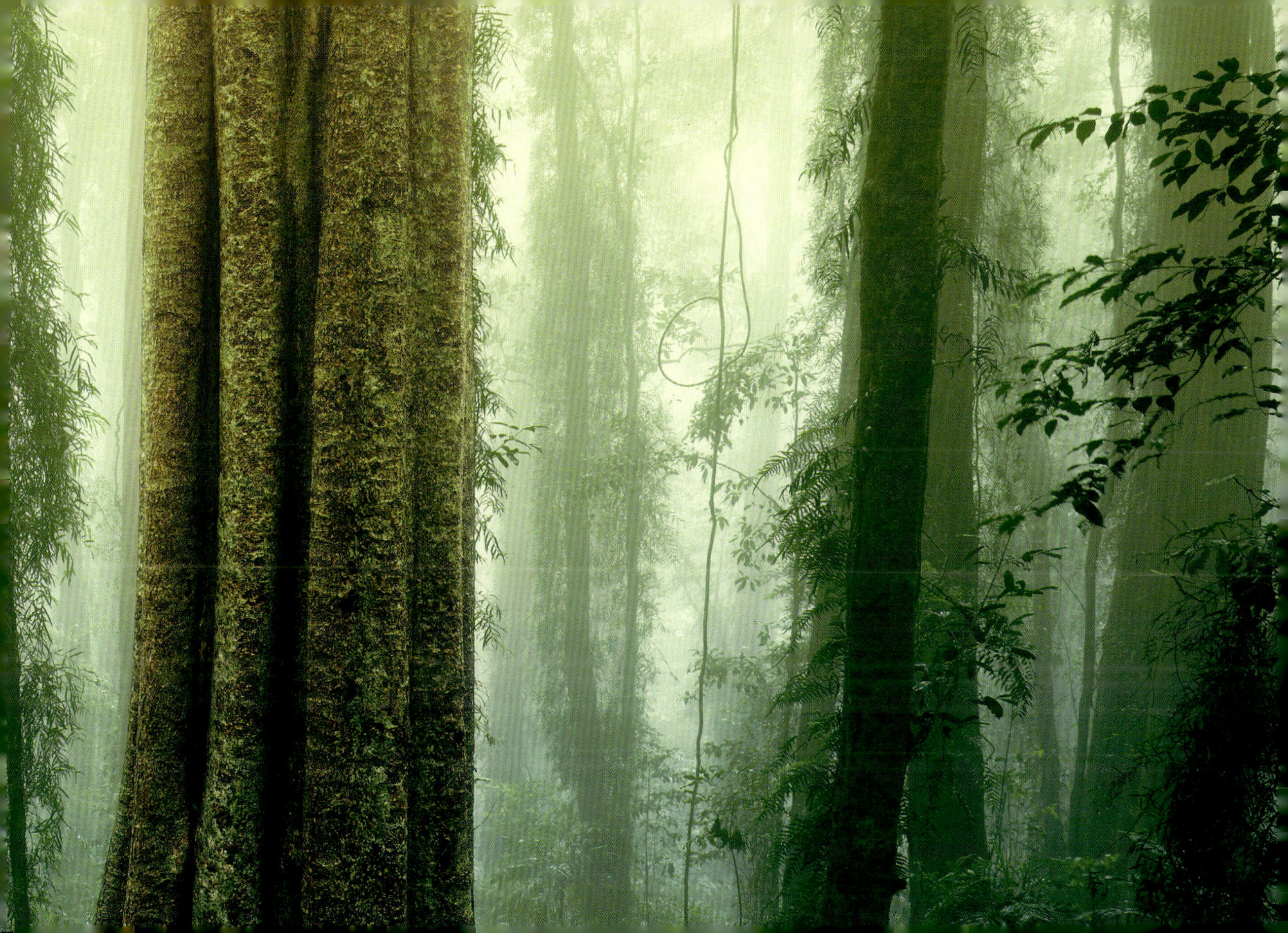

Hope is the prayer of the soul.

Dawn of Creation, Mitchell Falls, WA

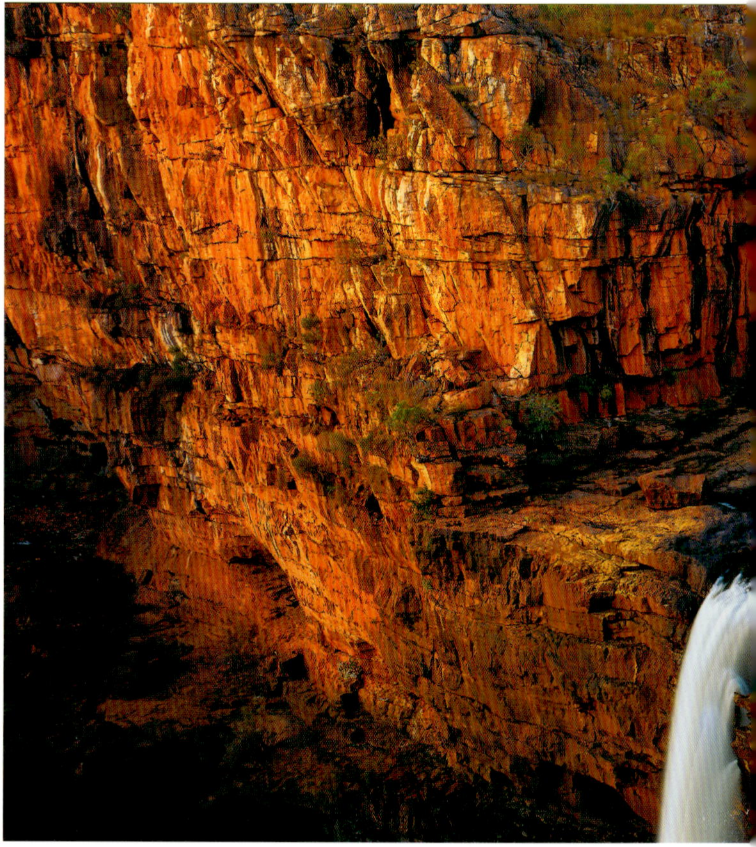

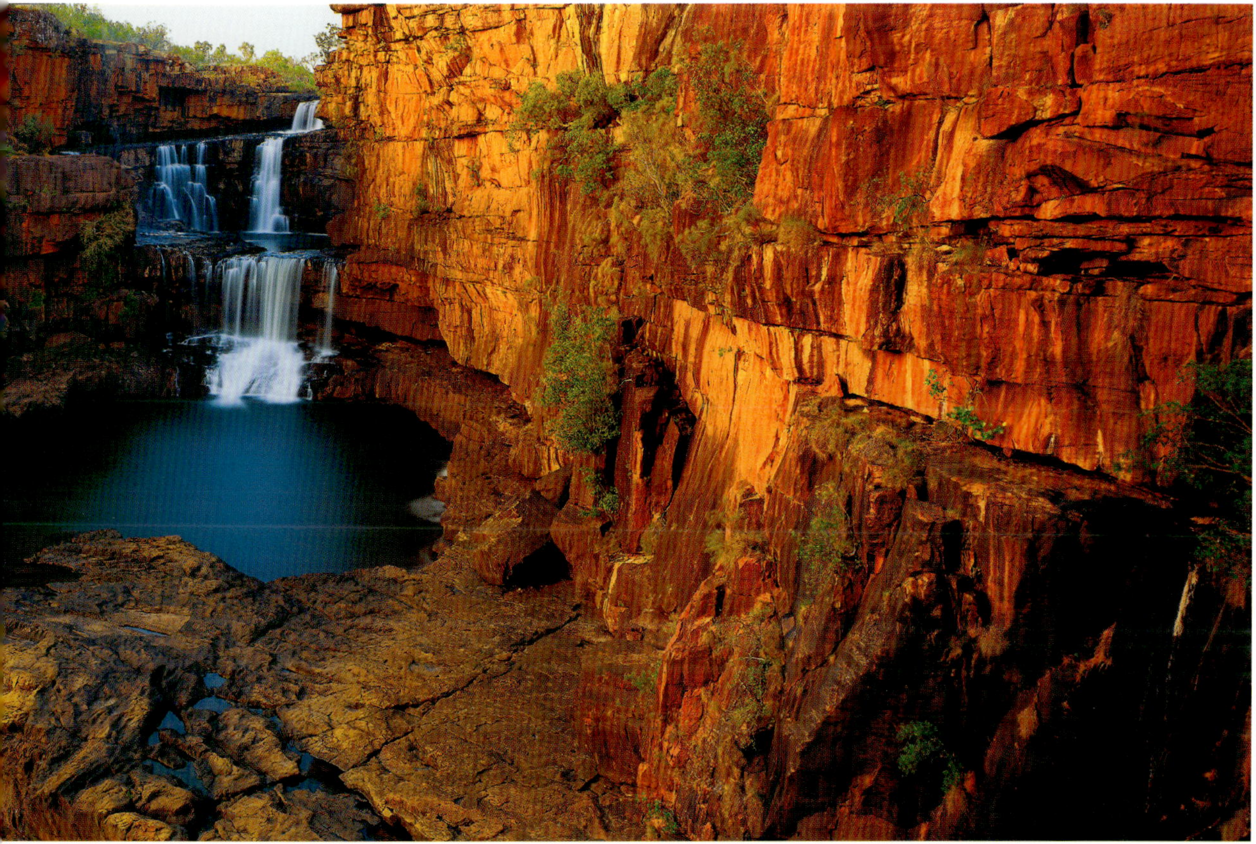

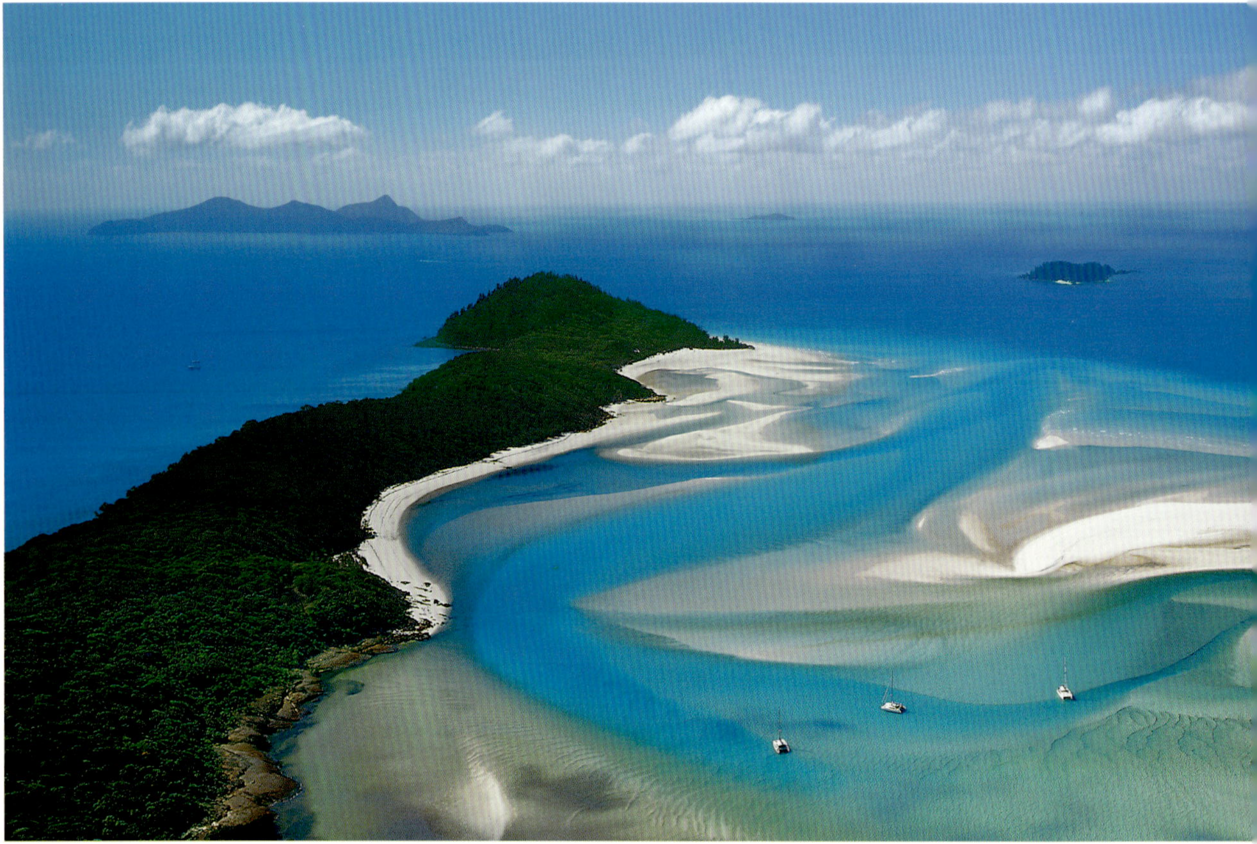

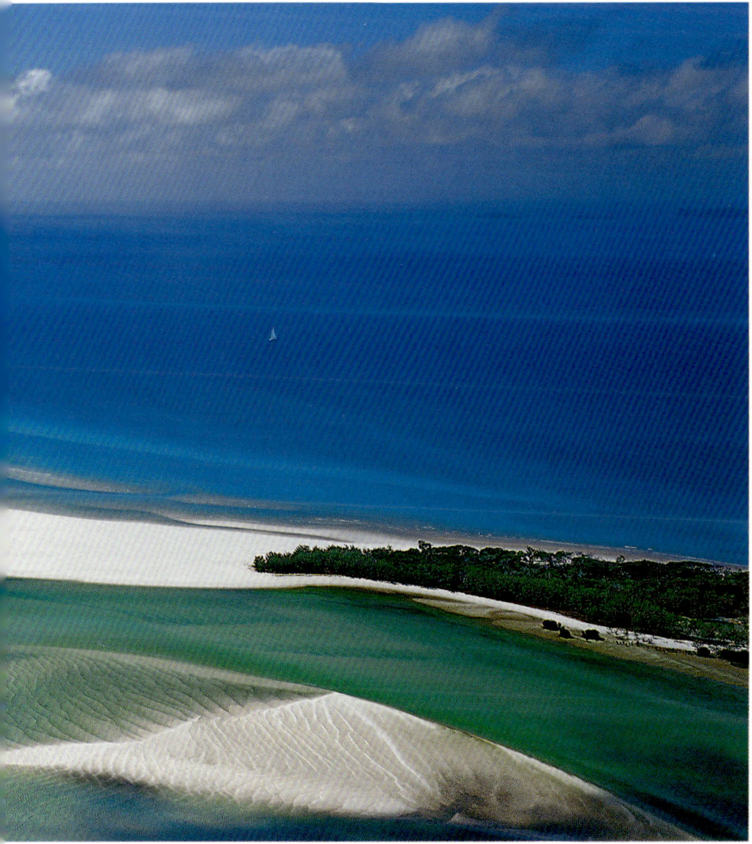

ISAIAH 40:28–31 NIV

Do you not know?

Have you not heard?

The LORD is the everlasting God,

the Creator of the ends of the earth.

He will not grow tired or weary, and his

understanding no one can fathom.

He gives strength to the weary and increases

the power of the weak. Even youths grow tired

and weary, and young men stumble and fall;

but those who hope in the LORD will renew

their strength. They will soar on wings like

eagles; they will run and not grow weary,

they will walk and not be faint.

Opal Waters, Whitsunday Island, Qld

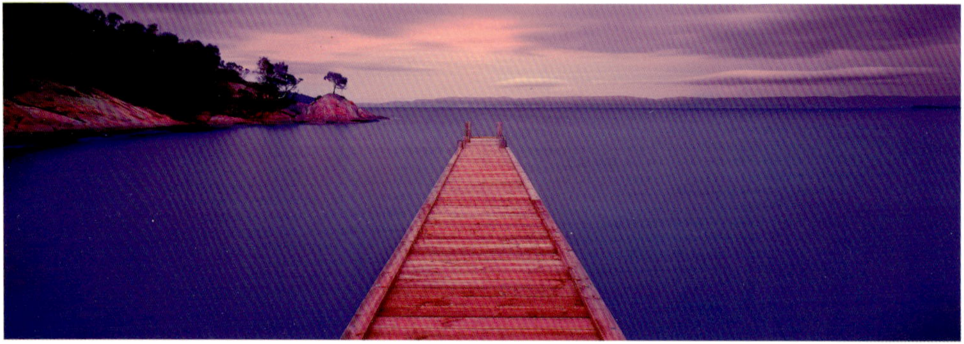

Peaceful Waters, Coles Bay, Tas

INSPIRATIONAL HOPE
First published 2011,
Reprinted 2017 and 2020
by Panographs Publishing Pty Ltd
ABN 21 050 235 606
PO Box 3015 Wamberal
NSW 2260 Australia
Telephone +61 2 4367 6777
Email: panos@kenduncan.com

Photography & text by Ken Duncan
©2020 Divine Guidance P/L
Designed by Good Catch Design
Reprographics by CFL Print Studio

Printed and bound in China

The National Library of Australia Cataloguing-in-Publication entry
Author: Duncan, Ken
Title: Inspirational hope: Australian photographs / by Ken Duncan
ISBN: 9780980834338 (hbk.)

Series: Inspirational books

Subjects:
Photography, Panoramic–Australia
Landscape photography–Australia
Hope–Quotations, maxims, etc
Australia–Pictorial works
Dewey Number: 778.360994

To view the range of Ken Duncan's Limited Edition Prints visit our Gallery:

**414 The Entrance Road,
Erina Heights, NSW
Telephone +61 2 4367 6701
Email: erina@kenduncan.com**

**Or shop online:
www.kenduncan.com**